Expository Nuggets
from the
Epistles

Stuart Briscoe Expository Outlines

D. Stuart Briscoe

Baker Books

A Division of Baker Book House Co
Grand Rapids, Michigan 49516

Published by Baker Books
a division of Baker Book House Company
P.O. Box 6287, Grand Rapids, MI 49516-6287

Printed in the United States of America

ISBN 0-8010-9007-5

Contents

Part 2: For People on the Grow: The Epistle to the Colossians

Part 3: Faith with Boots On: The Epistle of James

Part 4: When the Going Gets Tough: The First Epistle of Peter

Preface

Outlines and skeletons are quite similar. Sermons without outlines tend to "flop around" like bodies without bones. But bones without flesh are not particularly attractive; neither are outlines without development. The outlines presented in this book are nothing more than skeletal for a very good reason. I have no desire to produce ready-made sermons for pastors who need to develop their own, but on the other hand I recognize that many busy pastors who find sermon preparation time hard to come by may at least use them as a foundation for their own study, meditation, and preaching. They can add flesh to the bones; they can add development to structure. All the sermons based on these outlines have been preached during the last twenty-two years of my ministry at Elmbrook Church in Milwaukee, Wisconsin, and as one might expect, they vary in style and substance—not to mention quality! I trust, however, that they all seek to teach the Word and apply it to the culture to which they were preached, and if they help another generation of preachers as they "preach the Word" I will be grateful.

Part 1

A Transforming Letter

The Epistle to the Romans

1

An Apostle's Attitudes

Romans 1:1-17

There is no denying the remarkable impact of the apostle Paul's ministry on the first century nor its continued worldwide influence. Behind such outstanding achievement there lay powerful attitudes. What they were is easy to see.

I. Paul's realistic appraisal of himself (vv. 1–6)
   A. A ring of humility–"A servant *(doulos)* of Christ Jesus"
   B. A note of authority–"called to be an apostle"
   C. A sense of destiny–"set apart for the gospel" (Acts 13:2; Gal. 1:15)
   D. A feeling of adequacy–"received grace and apostleship"
   E. A life of ministry–"to call people . . . to belong . . ."

II. Paul's deep appreciation of his message
   A. The character of his message–"gospel"

    B. The confirmation of his message—"promised beforehand"

    C. The content of his message—"Jesus Christ our Lord"

       1. His humanity—"Seed of David"

       2. His deity—"Son of God"

         a. Declared with power

         b. Declared through the Spirit

         c. Declared by resurrection

    D. The consequences of his message

       1. There is power for salvation

         a. All powerful—"salvation" = "safe and sound"

         b. All embracing—"everyone who believes"

       2. There is righteousness revealed

         a. God is "in the right"

         b. God does what is right

         c. God makes us right with him

         d. God shows us how to live rightly (by faith)

III. Paul's profound affection for his people

    A. Encouragement

       1. Expressing appreciation—"your faith is being reported"

       2. Engaging in intercession—"constantly I remember you"

       3. Establishing in the faith—"mutually encouraged"

    B. Energy

       1. "I serve with my whole heart"

       2. "I pray the way may be opened"

    C. Enthusiasm

       1. "I am obligated"

       2. "I am eager"

       3. "I am not ashamed"

IV. Conclusion and application: Paul's attitudes help us understand his achievements. How do my attitudes compare?

2

First the Bad News

Romans 1:18-32

Gospel" means "good news," but to many people it clearly is not particularly good. The reason may be that they have not realized how bad the bad news is because they have overlooked the wrath of God.

I. The reality of the wrath of God
   A. An unavoidable biblical truth (v. 18; 1 Thess. 1:10)
   B. An unmistakable historical fact
   C. An undeniable moral necessity
      1. God's "rightness" requires it
      2. God's love reflects it
      3. Man's design assumes it
   D. An unpopular contemporary concept
      1. Rejecting plain teaching
      2. Misunderstanding true meaning

II. The reasons for the wrath of God
   A. Human attitudes toward God—"ungodliness"
   B. Human antipathy toward righteousness—"wickedness"
   C. Human activity against God
      1. Human suppression of truth
         a. Knowledge of God is plain

      b. Man is not ignorant–he is resistant
      c. Invisible has been made visible since creation (Acts 17:24–28)
      d. Man's resistance is inexcusable–he is accountable
  2. Human rejection of God
      a. Refusal to acknowledge God's glory
      b. Refusal to appreciate God's grace
      c. Fertile minds became futile
      d. Wisdom produced only folly
  3. Human substitution for truth
      a. The truth
         (1) God made man in his own image
         (2) God also created animals to be governed by man
      b. Human substitution
         (1) Man made God in his own image
         (2) Man then made God like the animals
         (3) Man totally reversed the order
         (4) Man substituted lies for truth
      c. Man worshiped creature and insulted Creator
  4. Human celebration of evil
      a. Man ignores divine reproof
      b. Man continues in disobedience
      c. Man delights in encouraging sin

III. The revelation of the wrath of God
  A. The wrath of God will be revealed (1 Thess. 1:10)
  B. The wrath of God is being revealed
    1. Man abused his God-given freedom
    2. So God "gave them over" to the consequences
    3. The results are confusion and corruption
      a. Spiritual
      b. Sexual
      c. Societal

IV. Conclusion: The wrath of God is revealed all around us–that's the bad news. The rightness of God is revealed in the gospel–that's the good news.

3

The Judgment of God

Romans 2:1-16

Paul's sweeping denunciation of human behavior no doubt stirred up indignant reaction in some of his hearers, as it still does today. By utilizing a literary device called diatribe–a debate with an anonymous person–he answers the objections and shows that everyone must face the judgment of God.

    I. The inconsistency of human judgment (v. 1)
        A. Human judgment is often necessary
        B. Human judgment is regularly practiced
        C. Human judgment is usually inconsistent
            1. Condemns the excessive and condones the moderate
            2. Indignant about action and ignorant of motive
            3. Easy to object and difficult to be objective
            4. Quick to be critical and slow to admit being hypocritical
        D. Human judgment is self-defeating

II. The integrity of divine judgment
Note: Paul declares divine judgment and does not debate
it
A. Divine judgment is just (v. 2)
   1. The judge is true
   2. The evidence is untainted
B. Divine judgment is inescapable (v. 3)
   1. No double standards
   2. No mistrial
   3. No exceptions
C. Divine judgment is cumulative (vv. 4–5)
   1. The coming judgment
   2. The divine kindness
   3. The human stubbornness
   4. The cumulative effect
D. Divine judgment is evaluative (vv. 6b–10)
   1. The God-seeker
      a. Motives
         (1) The glory of God–"glory"
         (2) The approval of God–"honor"
         (3) The presence of God–"immortality"
      b. Actions
         (1) Doing good
         (2) Persistence
      c. Evaluation–the gift of eternal life
   2. The self-seeker
      a. Motives
         (1) The enthronement of self
         (2) The dethronement of God
      b. Actions
         (1) Follows evil
         (2) Rejects truth
      c. Evaluation–wrath, anger, trouble, distress
E. Divine judgment is impartial (vv. 11–15)
   1. The privileged Jew
      a. Has the law to obey

      b. Will be judged by his obedience/disobedience

2. The underprivileged Gentile

      a. Does not have law

      b. Does have conscience

      c. Will be judged by the light he has

III. The inevitability of divine judgment (v. 16)

    A. God will judge

    B. Men's secrets will be judged

    C. The judgment will be by Christ

    D. This is the gospel

4

The Dangers of Religion

Romans 2:17–3:8

Having exposed the condition of pagan society, Roman and Greek, Paul turned his attention to the religious society of the Jewish people. Although he was a Jew, and proud of it, Paul did not hesitate to expose the spiritual danger inherent in religious profession.

I. The dangers of profession without performance (vv. 17–24)
   A. Profession (vv. 17–20)
      1. A special name—"call yourself a Jew"
      2. A special foundation—"rely on the law"
      3. A special relationship—"your relationship to God"
      4. A special insight—"you know his will . . ."
      5. A special conviction—"you are convinced . . ."
   B. Performance (vv. 21–24)
      1. Teaching without learning (v. 21a)
      2. Preaching without practicing (vv. 21b–22)
      3. Bragging without behaving (v. 23)

C. Possibilities
   1. Suffering from spiritual myopia
   2. Causing others to stumble
   3. Bringing dishonor to God's name

II. The dangers of ritual without reality (vv. 25–29)
   A. Ritual (v. 25a)
      1. The establishment of covenant (Gen. 17:10)
      2. The institution of circumcision
      3. The erosion of commitment (Deut. 10:12–22)
   B. Reality (Rom. 2:25b–29)
      1. External sign is no substitute for internal intention
      2. External sign gives no freedom for unfaithfulness
      3. External sign in flesh portrays inner work of Spirit
   C. Repercussions
      1. Circumcised lawbreakers are condemned by uncircumcised pagans
      2. Uncircumcised pagans who obey receive God's praise
      3. Circumcised lawbreakers receive man's praise (Note: "Judah" = "praise")

III. The dangers of privilege without perception (3:1–2)
   A. The danger of abusing privilege–"the very words of God"
   B. The danger of disregarding responsibility
   C. The danger of exaggerating personal importance

IV. The dangers of objections without objectivity (3:3–8)
   A. Objections
      1. If the religious are so bad, how can they still be privileged?
      2. If they aren't still privileged, God is unfaithful
      3. If our sin proves his justice, he is using us
      4. We may as well sin more and make God look better!

B. Objectivity
   1. Objectivity requires an acknowledgment of sin
   2. Objectivity demands a recognition of hypocrisy
   3. Objectivity projects a reverence of God

V. Conclusions: Pagans suppress what they know of God.
   Religious know more but still come short.

5

All Together Now

Romans 3:9-20

The human race is severely fragmented. No one denies it, although many ignore it, and some look for common ground on which some semblance of unity might be built. Paul states the common ground that is largely overlooked but that, if properly appreciated, could work wonders.

I. All under sin
  A. The conclusion (v. 9)
    "Religious" sinners are no better than "irreligious" sinners
  B. The charge (vv. 10–18)
    1. Sin–a factor that must not be ignored
      a. Sins are fruits
      b. Sin is root
    2. Sin–a force that cannot be dismissed
      a. All under sin's control
      b. All under sin's condemnation
    3. Sin–a fault that will not go away
      a. A fault running through human character
        (1) Spiritual declension–"none righteous"

       (2) Intellectual deprivation–"none under-
          stands"
       (3) Volitional disinclination–"none seeks"
       (4) Moral deviation–"all gone out of the way"
       (5) Social destruction–"none does good"
   b. A fault running through human conduct
       (1) Throats like open tombs
       (2) Tongues practiced in deceit
       (3) Lips paralyzing with poison
       (4) Mouths full of bitterness
       (5) Feet rushing to violence
       (6) Eyes unfocused toward God
   c. A fault running through the human condition
       (1) Their path is strewn with ruin
       (2) Their pursuit of peace is futile
       (3) Their pride dismisses God

II. All under law (v. 19)
  A. The law–Moses; the Old Testament–Jews
  B. The law is written on the heart–Gentiles (2:15)
  C. The law shuts every mouth
  D. The law finds everyone guilty

III. All under pressure (3:20)
  A. Humanity is incapable of deserving justification
  B. Humanity is inexcusable because it understands sin
  C. Humanity is inescapably dependent on divine grace

IV. Conclusion: Human solidarity is found in common sin-
fulness, guilt, and need. Denial of this leads to further
disunity.

6

The Genius of God

Romans 3:21-31

We have now reached one of the pivotal points of the epistle, introduced by the words "But now . . ." After the powerful charge that "all are under sin" and merit divine judgment, Paul begins to outline God's answer to the human predicament.

I. The divine dilemma
  A. The human condition (v. 23)
    1. All have sinned—archer's arrow
    2. All have come short—lagging runner
    3. Every mouth is silenced (v. 19)
  B. The divine character
    1. He is righteous—"righteousness," "justice," "just" all related (v. 21)
    2. He is gracious (v. 24)
  C. The crucial issue: How can God "be just and the one who justifies"? (v. 26; e.g., John 8)

II. The universal solution
    A. Justification—language of the law court
        1. To be declared righteous in God's court
        2. Freely by his grace (Rom. 3:24)
        3. Not by observing the law (v. 20)
    B. Redemption—language of the marketplace
        1. To be ransomed by paying a price
        2. Came by Christ Jesus (v. 24)
        3. Not by silver and gold (1 Peter 1:18)
    C. Propitiation—language of the temple
        1. To placate wrath
        2. In his blood
            Note: *Hilasterion*—mercy seat
        3. Through faith

III. The common denominators
    A. No room for racial pride—all justified the same way
    B. No place for arrogant boasting—no one justified by law
    C. No exception to way of salvation—justification by grace through faith

7

Facing Up to Faith

Romans 4:1-25

We have all been taught that there is no such thing as a free lunch, but that does not mean that nothing is free–it means that if something is given freely somebody footed the bill. So it is with salvation; but man has to believe that salvation is free because God paid the price.

  I. The father of faith (vv. 1–4)
     A. Abraham's exemplary life (Gen. 26:5)
     B. But Abraham cannot boast before God
     C. Because he was reckoned righteous by faith

 II. The forgiveness of faith (Rom. 4:5–8)
     A. Works produce wages
     B. Faith receives gifts
     C. Imputed righteousness is "blessedness"
     D. Because:
        1. Transgressions are forgiven
        2. Sins are covered
        3. Man is not held accountable

III. The family of faith (vv. 9–16)
    A. Abraham–father of the Jews through Isaac
    B. Abraham–father of the Arabs through Ishmael
    C. Abraham–"father of us all" through faith
       1. Circumcision is not determining factor
          a. Abraham justified fourteen years before circumcision
          b. Abraham justified–circumcision the seal
       2. Law is not determining factor
          a. Abraham justified 430 years before law was given
          b. Law teaches sinfulness of sin
          c. Law is mirror but not soap
       3. Faith is determining factor
          a. Circumcised/uncircumcised believers are justified
          b. Circumcised/uncircumcised unbelievers are not

IV. The factors of faith (vv. 17–25)
    A. Faith–confidence in a person (vv. 17–18)
       1. God gives life to death
       2. God calls existence out of nothing
    B. Faith–conversant with problems (v. 19)
       1. He faced the facts
       2. He applied his faith
    C. Faith–consistent in progress (v. 20)
       1. Delays and disappointments were his lot
       2. They served only to strengthen
    D. Faith–convinced of the promises (v. 21)
       1. Divine integrity–he promised
       2. Divine ability–he was able (e.g., v. 25)

 V. Conclusion: This was not only for Abraham but for us (v. 24).

8

Good Christian Men and Women, Rejoice

Romans 5:1-11

Celebration and depression seem to be commonplace in our world. The former is often related to a mindless, unthinking irresponsibility, while the latter is connected to a hopelessness that sees no solutions to life's problems. What should be the Christian's attitude? We should rejoice intelligently.

   I. Rejoice in your present position (vv. 1–2a)
      A. Justified through faith
      B. Peace with God
      C. Standing in grace

  II. Rejoice in your future prospects (v. 2b)
      A. The anxiety of uncertainty
      B. The celebration of confidence

 III. Rejoice in your personal problems (vv. 3–5)
      A. Rejoicing through knowing . . .
      B. Pressures produce perseverance . . .
      C. Perseverance produces character . . .

   D. Character produces confidence . . .
   E. Confidence is not misplaced . . .
   F. Because a loving God is in control

IV. Rejoice in your spiritual possessions (vv. 6–10)
   A. Human need
      1. What we are–sinners, ungodly, powerless, enemies
      2. What we did–omission, commission
      3. Where we are heading–wrath of God
   B. Divine action
      1. Loved us while yet sinners
      2. Christ died for us:
         a. Justified by his blood–deals with what we did
         b. Saved from wrath–deals with where we're heading
         c. Saved by his life–deals with what we are

 V. Rejoice in God's person (v. 11)
   A. Through the Lord Jesus Christ . . .
   B. We have received reconciliation . . .
   C. Because of who he is and what he did

VI. Conclusion: Christians should always be ready to celebrate.

9

The Four Monarchs

Romans 5:12-21

It may have occurred to Paul that he had written much about sin in individual lives without describing either the vast extent of sin's domination or how sin came to be such a problem in the first place. He used the word "reign" to describe sin's domination but balanced the expressions by talking about four monarchs.

  I. The reign of sin
   A. Sin entered (v. 12)
     1. Through one man—Adam
       a. Breaking a command (v. 14)
       b. Trespass (v. 15)
       c. Disobedience (v. 19)
       d. Judgment (v. 16)
       e. Condemnation (v. 16)
   B. Sin increased (v. 20)
     1. Through adding the law (v. 20; also vv. 13–14)
     2. The many were made sinners (v. 19)
       a. Federal headship—Adam acting on behalf of all
       b. Natural headship—Adam was the race and the race is Adam

Note: corporate personality; e.g., Einstein's *Nuclear Age,* Donne's *No Man Is an Island*
C. Sin reigned (v. 21)
   1. Dominating all people
   2. Permeating all things

II. The reign of death
   A. Death entered
      1. Through sin (v. 12)
      2. Physical
      3. Spiritual
      4. Eternal
   B. Death reigned
      1. Before the law (v. 14)
      2. Came to all men (v. 12)

III. The reign of grace
   A. Grace entered
      1. Adam contrasted with Christ (v. 14)
      2. Trespass contrasted with gift (v. 15)
      3. Death contrasted with life (vv. 16–17)
      4. Condemnation contrasted with justification (v. 16)
      5. Disobedience contrasted with obedience (vv. 18–19)
         Note: contrast Albert Einstein and Alexander Fleming. The former introduced us to the nuclear age, the latter to the age of penicillin. They were contemporaries.
   B. Grace reigned
      1. Sin increased, grace increased all the more (v. 20)
      2. Grace overflowed to the many (v. 15)

IV. The reign of life
   A. Those who receive abundant provision . . .
   B. And the gift of righteousness . . .
   C. Reign in life by Jesus Christ

V. Conclusion: Powerful forces are at work, but believers through Christ triumph.

10

Should Saints Sin?

Romans 6:1-23

Richard Lovelace wrote in his book, *Dynamics of Spiritual Life,* "Three aberrations from the Biblical teaching on justification— cheap grace, legalism and moralism—still dominate the church today." Paul, in this passage, turns his attention to the first-century equivalent of "cheap grace."

I. Saints' relationship to sin
   A. Moralist
      1. Man's effort without God
      2. Sanctification without justification
   B. Legalist
      1. Application of rules
      2. Imposition of disciplines
   C. Cheap grace
      1. If grace abounds where sin abounds . . .
      2. Let's keep grace flowing by sinning more
   D. None of the above!—"We died to sin"

II. Saints' relationship to Christ
   A. Baptism into Christ (v. 3)
      1. Gentile proselyte to Judaism

      2. Jewish/Gentile convert to Christ
      3. External sign of internal grace
      4. Termination of the old
      5. Initiation of the new
      6. Identification with Christ
   B. With Christ in death, and resurrection (vv. 3–5)
      1. Our Christ died and rose again
      2. We, united to him, share his death and resurrection
   C. Christ died to sin, rose to live anew (vv. 6–11)
      1. In his death he dealt thoroughly with sin
         a. He fully paid its penalty
         b. He totally overthrew its power–death
      2. In his resurrection he lived again free
   D. We died and live again in him
      1. One who has died is freed (justified) from sin (v. 7)
      2. Old self was crucified (v. 6)
      3. Body of sin rendered powerless
      4. No longer slaves
      5. Now obligated to new living

III. Saints' relationship to temptation
   A. Temptation continues, failure still possible but:
   B. Reckoning is necessary (v. 11)
      1. Dead to sin
      2. Alive to God
   C. Denying is necessary (v. 12)
      1. Recognize evil desires
      2. Say "no"
   D. Yielding is necessary (v. 13)
      1. Recognize righteousness
      2. Say "yes"

IV. Saints' relationship to righteousness
   A. The old slavery to sin and its fruits has ended
   B. The new slavery to righteousness and its fruits has begun

11

What about the Law?

Romans 7:1-25

Paul's statement "You are not under law but under grace," while wonderfully true, is often woefully misunderstood and misapplied. This section examines the believer's relationship to the law.

I. The believer's release from the law (vv. 1–6)
   A. An illustration (vv. 1–3)
      1. The law of marriage
      2. The release from law
   B. An application (vv. 4–6)
      1. Mr. Law is holy (v. 12), good (v. 13), spiritual (v. 14), demanding (Gal. 3:10)
      2. Mrs. Law is frustrated, humiliated (Rom. 7:5)
      3. Mr. Law dies (analogy convoluted!)
      4. Mrs. Law is free to remarry
      5. Mrs. Law becomes Mrs. Risen-from-Dead (v. 6)

II. The believer's respect for the law (v. 7)
   A. Law cannot reproduce righteousness

B. Law can expose sin
C. Law does reveal inner realities

III. The believer's revelation through the law (vv. 8–13)
   A. The law stands for holiness, justice, and goodness
   B. This is life
   C. "This do and you shall live"–principle of operation
   D. Not doing brings death–unholy, unjust, not good
   E. Sin has been unmasked

IV. The believer's relationship to the law (vv. 14–25)
   A. Awareness of condition (vv. 14, 18)
      1. Carnal, sin-enslaved in contrast to law (v. 14)
      2. Carnality incapable of spirituality (v. 18)
   B. Acknowledgment of conflict (vv. 15, 18–19)
      1. Puzzlement and disappointment (v. 15)
      2. Ambivalence and contradiction (vv. 18–19)
   C. Arrival at conclusion (vv. 17, 20–25)
      1. Since I have a sensitivity to holiness . . .
      2. And a proclivity to ungodliness . . .
      3. I am a battleground
         a. I am wretched
         b. I am in need of help
         c. I know where to find it
         d. I am aware the conflict will persist
         e. I know that through the Spirit there is triumph

V. Application
   A. Legalists need to recognize law reveals sin and leads to Christ
   B. Antinomians need to acknowledge law is good, man is sinful
   C. Believers need to remember the conflict continues but the Spirit enables

12

The Three Spiritual Laws

Romans 8:1-13

Paul frequently used the expression "in Christ Jesus" (vv. 1–2). To be "in Christ Jesus" means to have a vital faith relationship with the crucified and risen Christ. Great benefits and responsibilities accrue to those who enjoy such a relationship.

I. Benefit #1—no condemnation (v. 1)
   A. Condemnation passed upon all (5:18)
   B. Now no condemnation (8:1)
   C. Because God condemned sin in the flesh (v. 3)
      1. He did what the law could not do
      2. He did it in his Son
      3. He sent him in likeness of sinful flesh
      4. He sent him for sin (offering)

II. Benefit #2—no bondage (v. 2)
    Note: the three spiritual laws
    A. The law of sin and death
       1. The law of sin at work in my members (7:23)
       2. The flesh a slave to the law of sin (7:25)

    3. Living according to the flesh leads to sin and death (8:5)
    4. The flesh has a mind-set (v. 5)
    5. This mind-set is death, hostile, incapable (vv. 6–7)
    6. This lifestyle cannot please God (v. 8)
B. The law of the Spirit of life
    1. "In Christ" the law of the Spirit operates (v. 2)
    2. The Spirit is stronger than the flesh (v. 9)
    3. The Spirit is evidence of belonging to Christ (v. 9)
    4. The Spirit of him who raised Jesus lives in us (vv. 10–11)
    5. There is a Spirit mind-set (v. 6)
    6. This mind-set produces life and peace (v. 6)
C. The law of fulfilled righteousness; e.g., the law of aerodynamics in an airplane sets me free from the law of gravity
    1. Observation–set free (v. 2)
    2. Obligation–debtors (v. 13)
    3. Operation
        a. Minding (vv. 5–6)
        b. Walking (v. 4)
        c. Mortifying (v. 13)

13

Living in the Spirit

Romans 8:14-27

Having explained in principle what happens when believers receive the "Spirit of him who raised Jesus from the dead," Paul now leads into a practical explanation of life in the Spirit.

I. Living in the good of the family (vv. 14–17)
Note family words: sons, children, adoption, heirs, "*Abba* Father"
A. The experience of the leading of the Spirit (v. 14)
Note: "The Spirit drags the man where the flesh would fain not go." (Godet)
1. An evidence of sonship
2. Obligation of sons to be led
3. Alert to prompting, obedient to control (e.g., Luke 4:1)
B. The experience of liberty through the Spirit (Rom. 8:15a)
1. Fear creates bondage

        2. Spirit gives freedom (e.g., 2 Tim. 1:7)

   C. The experience of life in the Spirit (Rom. 8:15a)

        1. The ministry of adoption–status, privilege by choice

        2. *Abba*–Aramaic expression of endearment (e.g., Mark. 14:36)

   D. The experience of learning from the Spirit (Rom. 8:16–17)

        1. Learning "with our spirit"

        2. Learning about status as sons

        3. Learning about sharing as heirs

        4. Learning about suffering as normative

  II. Living in the midst of futility (vv. 18–22)

   A. Creation subjected to futility, decay, pain, because of man

   B. Creation will be redeemed when man is freed

   C. Creation eagerly awaits that day

 III. Living in the light of the futurity (vv. 23–27)

   A. We have "firstfruits," but we groan

   B. We are "saved," but still await redemption

   C. We pray, but don't know what to say

   D. But the Spirit intercedes . . .

   E. And the Father understands . . .

   F. And we persevere in hope

14

What Shall We Say?

Romans 8:28-39

At this point the tone of the epistle changes. Having carefully and systematically laid out his theological statement, the apostle now adopts a preaching style and, with a series of questions, he asks for a response. This response should include the following:

I. We are more than convinced (vv. 28–30)
   A. That God has a plan
      1. Man made in God's image (Gen. 1:26)
      2. Man reproduced in his own image (5:3)
      3. Christ came in God's image (Heb. 1:3)
      4. He will be "firstborn" of those conformed to his image (Rom. 8:29)
      5. "We shall be like him" (1 John 3:2)
   B. That God has a procedure
      1. Those he foreknew he predestined . . . (Rom. 8:29)
         a. Divine foreknowledge
            (1) To know in advance what people will do
            (2) To know intimately some people and not others
         b. Divine predestination

           (1) Determining in advance what the fore-
                known would become
           (2) Sovereignly deciding limits of human
                experience
    2. Those he predestined he called . . . (v. 30)
      a. Divine intervention in human affairs
      b. Divine invitation (calling, summons) to share
    3. Those he called he justified . . . (v. 30)
    4. Those he justified he glorified . . . (v. 30)
      a. "Sanctification is glory begun . . ."
      b. ". . . Glory is sanctification completed." (F. F.
      Bruce)
  C. That God has made a promise (v. 28)
    1. His plan stretches from eternity to eternity
    2. His commitment is to the ultimate good

II. We are more than conquerors (vv. 31–37)
  A. Conquering opposition (v. 31)
    1. Who can be against us?
    2. If God is for us
  B. Conquering inadequacy (v. 32)
    1. Who will give us what we need?
    2. God did not spare his Son
  C. Conquering fear (v. 33)
    1. Who is going to charge us?
    2. God has justified
  D. Conquering uncertainty (v. 34)
    1. Who is going to condemn us?
    2. Christ intercedes for us
  E. Conquering life (vv. 35–37)
    1. All life's disruptive eventualities . . .
    2. Are to be expected . . .
    3. And overcome through him who loves us

III. We are more than confident (vv. 38–39)
  A. Of God's love
  B. Of God's superiority
  C. Of Christ being "our Lord"

15

Israel's Rejection of Christ

Romans 9:1-33

Paul's presentation of the gospel of Christ was not at all acceptable to many Jews for obvious reasons. As a result, the veracity of his message and his own credibility were under fire. More than that, profound questions concerning election and rejection needed to be answered. They still do.

I. The servant of God is intense
    A. Paul's sincere concern is evident (v. 1)
    B. Paul's delight is tinged with anguish (v. 2)
    C. Paul's intense feelings are displayed (v. 3)
    D. Paul's appreciation for Israel is on record (vv. 4-5)
       Note: In all this intensity of feeling, three things are clear:

II. The word of God is not invalidated (vv. 6-13)
    Note: "Word of God"–his plan or purpose
    A. God called Abram, not Terah

  B. God chose Isaac, not Ishmael

  C. God differentiated between Israel (natural) and Israel (spiritual)

  D. God sees children of promise and natural children differently

  E. God "loved" Jacob and "hated" Esau

    1. Note: peoples, not individuals (Mal. 1:2–3)

    2. Note: hyperbolic expression (Luke 14:26)

  F. Nothing has changed by Israel's reaction

III. The sovereignty of God is illuminated (Rom. 9:14–19)
Note: Some Jews believed that to be the "chosen people" was an eternal guarantee and not to be the chosen people guaranteed an unblessed state. For Paul to teach otherwise was, to them, to make God act unjustly.

  A. Is God unrighteous?

  B. No—he is just to all

  C. He chooses to be merciful; e.g., Moses (Exod. 33:19)

  D. He chooses to harden; e.g., Pharaoh (9:16)
Note: Pharaoh's repeated hardening

IV. The consistency of God is illustrated (Rom. 9:20–33)

  A. God is consistent in his dealings

    1. He is not deterred by his creatures' objections (vv. 20–21)

    2. He is not bound by any man-made restrictions (vv. 22–24)

  B. God is consistent in his devotion (vv. 25–29)

    1. Devoted to his people

    2. Devoted to his principles

      a. There will always be a remnant, which God preserves

      b. There will always be rebellion, which God resists

  C. God is consistent in his determination (vv. 30–33)

    1. No one is justified by keeping the law

    2. Anyone who receives grace by faith is justified

    3. Christ is the issue . . .

    4. He's either a stumbling stone or the bedrock

Thought: Too often we look at God through man's eyes. Here he lets us take a peek through his eyes. The result?

16

The Importance of Evangelism

Romans 10:1-21

Paul's discussion of divine sovereignty and human accountability, with particular reference to Israel, tends to go over people's heads, but it serves an essentially practical purpose. Paul, the theologian, was always a lover of people and a deeply committed evangelist.

  I. Evangelism–the exposure of error (vv. 1-4)
   A. The delicate task of exposing error (vv. 1-2)
     1. A genuine concern for people–"my heart's desire"
     2. A humble reliance on divine aid–"prayer to God"
     3. A deep understanding of the other position–"I can testify about them"
     4. A careful diagnosis of the situation–"zeal but not knowledge"
   B. The specific errors that should be exposed (vv. 3-4)
     1. A false impression of God–"God's righteousness"

2. An erroneous understanding of man–"own righteousness"
3. An inaccurate view of Christ–"Christ is the end of the law"

II. Evangelism–the exposition of truth (vv. 5–13)
   A. Contrast (vv. 5–8)
      1. What law requires
      2. What grace offers
   B. Conviction–"believe in your heart"
   C. Confession–"Jesus is Lord"
   D. Confidence
      1. Believe and be justified
      2. Confess and be saved

III. Evangelism–the exercise of faith (vv. 14–21)
   A. The experience of believers
      1. Everyone who calls will be saved
      2. Calling requires believing
      3. Believing requires hearing
      4. Hearing requires telling
      5. Telling requires sending
   B. The experience of unbelievers
      1. Have they not heard?
      2. Have they not understood?
      3. Have they disobeyed?

17

God and Israel

Romans 11:1-36

The old hymn says, "God works in mysterious ways his wonders to perform." Nowhere is this better illustrated than in his dealings with Israel. His ways are wonderful, and the appropriate response is wonder and adoration.

I. God's preservation of a remnant in Israel (vv. 1–10)
  A. God has not rejected his people
    1. The evidence of Paul
      a. A son of Abraham
      b. Of the tribe of Benjamin
      c. Named for Benjamin's most famous person
      d. So long as there are Pauls, God has not rejected his people
  B. God has preserved a remnant
    1. The example of Elijah
      a. The apostasy in Elijah's time
      b. Elijah's courageous and lonely stand
      c. The silent 7,000
      d. Always a nucleus honoring the Lord

    C. God has acted against the rejecters
       1. Moral insensitivity
       2. Spiritual numbness

  II. God's purpose in the rejection of Israel (vv. 11–15)
    A. Israel's rejection of Christ
       1. A stumbling for Israel
       2. An opportunity for Gentiles
    B. God's rejection of Israel
       1. The fall means universal blessing
       2. What will their recovery mean?

 III. God's power with regard to Israel (vv. 16–25)
    A. God's power to continue what he started
       1. Firstfruits and batch
       2. Root and branches
    B. God's power to adapt
       1. Fruitless branches broken off
       2. Wild branches grafted in
    C. God's power to control
       1. Arrogance and reverence
       2. Kindness and sternness

 IV. God's promise of restoration for Israel (vv. 26–36)
    A. God is faithful to his promises
    B. God is committed to his remnant
    C. God is completing his work
    D. God will bring revival to Israel
    E. God has universal blessing in mind

Thought: What should our response be to this exposition of the Gospel? See Romans 11:33–36.

18

A Sense of Values

Romans 12:1-8

"Therefore, I urge you, brothers . . ." begins the final section of this great epistle. It introduces a heartfelt, brotherly appeal to a practical application of the truth and gets right into the heart of spiritual experience by urging the readers to evaluate their values in the light of all that has been explained so far.

    I. The reality of your commitment (vv. 1-2)
        A. The requests
            1. Offer your bodies
                a. "Offer"–sacrifice, offering
                b. "Bodies"–the whole person as expressed in physical environment
                c. "Living"–life is the sphere in which spirituality is expressed
                d. "Holy"–as opposed to body as instrument of sin
                e. "Acceptable"–like Abel, unlike Cain
            2. Do not conform
                a. "This world"–as opposed to the world to come
                b. "Conform"–don't be pressed into a mold

      3. Be transformed
        a. "Transformed"–metamorphosis
        b. "Renewed mind"–the means of transformation
    B. The reasons
      1. "The mercies of God"–see previous 11 chapters!
      2. "Therefore"–see previous verse!
      3. "Reasonable service"–spiritual worship
    C. The results
      1. The will of God discovered
      2. The plan of God proven

II. The estimation of yourself (v. 3)
    A. Don't overestimate yourself
    B. Do properly evaluate yourself
      1. The gifts he has given
      2. The faith (power, ability) he has measured out

III. The functions of your church (vv. 4–5)
    A. The believer's place in the body
    B. The diversity of ability in the body
    C. The necessity for coordination and cooperation in the body

IV. The exercise of your gifts (vv. 6–8)
    A. Gifts are according to grace that is given
    B. Gifts differ according to the Spirit's intention
    C. Gifts to be exercised need appropriate attitudes
      1. Prophecy requires faith
      2. Serving requires action
      3. Teaching requires communicating
      4. Encouraging requires getting alongside
      5. Giving requires generosity
      6. Leadership requires diligence
      7. Mercy requires cheerfulness

19

Good and Evil

Romans 12:9-21

Having dealt with evil on the cosmic scale, Paul now turns to a practical treatment of evil in the life of the individual. Showing how evil is found in attitudes as well as actions, he teaches believers how to shun evil and embrace good.

   I. Good, evil, and fellowship (vv. 9-12)
      A. Attitudes (v. 9)
         1. Love characterized by sincerity
         2. Evil hated with intensity
         3. Good embraced with tenacity
      B. Activities (vv. 10-12)
         1. Relationships (v. 10)
            a. Devotion to each other
            b. Respect for each other
         2. Responsibilities (v. 11)
            a. Approach them with enthusiasm
            b. Fulfill them with spiritual delight
            c. Accept them as service to the Lord (times?)
               Note: *Kurios* = Lord, *Kairos* = times

3. Reactions (v. 12)
   a. Discouragement–the joy of hope
   b. Opposition–patience
   c. Opportunity–faithfulness in prayer

II. Good, evil, and stewardship (vv. 13–16)
    A. Attitudes
       1. The recognition of resources
       2. The use and abuse of resources
    B. Activities
       1. Resources–economic assets (v. 13)
          a. Meeting specific needs
          b. Sharing heart and hearth
       2. Resources–Christ's example (v. 14)
          a. How he handled persecution
          b. How we follow his example (1 Peter 2:23)
       3. Resources–community life (Rom. 12:15–16)
          a. Genuine empathy (v. 15)
          b. Genuine acceptance–harmony
          c. Genuine humility

III. Good, evil, and hardship
     A. Attitudes
        1. Retaliation–evil for evil (v. 17)
        2. Revenge–"getting even" (v. 19)
     B. Activities
        1. Doing what is right (v. 17)
        2. Working toward peace (v. 18)
           a. If possible
           b. As it depends on you
        3. Leaving God room to work (v. 19)
        4. Killing enemies with kindness (v. 20)
        5. Overcoming rather than overcome (v. 21)

20

The Christian Attitude toward Authority

Romans 13:1-7

Having dealt with the Christian's behavior in the church, Paul turns his attention to the way a person with a renewed mind functions in a secular society, with particular reference to his response to governmental authority.

I. The principles of authority (vv. 1–2)
  A. God's authority demonstrated
    1. In creation (4:17)
    2. In legislation
      a. The law given (2:12–13)
      b. The consequences determined (1:24, 26, 28)
      c. The ultimate jurisdiction (3:19)
    3. In resurrection (1:4)
  B. God's authority delegated
    1. To Christ (2:16; see Acts 17:31)
    2. To parents (Eph. 6:1–3), church leaders (Heb. 13:7, 17)
    3. To governing authorities (Rom. 13:1)
      a. Man is to live in societies

      b. Societies need authorities to maintain order
      c. God has ordained this (see Acts 23:10–11)
      d. To resist is to resist what God established

II. The purpose of authority (Rom. 13:3–4)
    Note: Preamble to Constitution of U.S.A.
    A. Rulers as God's servants (vv. 4, 6)
      Note: Greek *Leitourgos* (15:16, 27; Heb. 8:2)
    B. Rulers as encouragers of good (see also 1 Peter 2:13–14)
      1. To command
      2. To do good (see 1 Tim. 2:2)
      3. To protect
    C. Rulers as punishers of evil
      1. Holding terror for wrongdoers
      2. Bearing the sword (not for nothing!)
      3. (God's) agent of wrath
    D. Rulers as governors (Rom. 13:6–7)
      1. To fully govern
      2. To finance by taxation

III. The problems of authority
    A. The necessity of submission (v. 5)
      1. Submission to regulation
      2. Acceptance of punishment
    B. The exercise of conscience
      1. Developing a sense of what is "right"
      2. Is it right to dissent? (see Acts 5:29)
      3. Is it right to resist? (see Matt. 22:21)
      4. Is it right to rebel?
        a. Against the expenditure of taxes?
        b. Against the use or abuse of the sword?
        c. Against the deification of the state?

21

Rouse to Reality

Romans 13:8-14

It is surprising to discover that Paul evidently thought that the readers of his letter had dozed off, because he found it necessary to tell them it was time they woke of their slumber. That it was a spiritual sleeping sickness is illustrated by the Amplified New Testament translation—"rouse to reality."

    I. The reality of practical obligation (vv. 8–10)
      A. Obligations to governments (v. 7)
      B. Obligations to creditors
      C. Obligations to neighbors
        1. Love as obligation
          a. Not noble ideal
          b. Not optional extra
        2. Love as fulfilling the law
          a. Impossible in flesh (7:7–13)
          b. Possible in the Spirit (8:4)
        3. Love as demonstrated in self-concern
          a. My safety
          b. My security

    c. My sustenance

    d. My station

  4. Love as applied to my neighbor
Is the opposite of:

    a. Adultery

    b. Murder

    c. Robbery

    d. Deception

    e. Envy

II. The reality of eternal orientation (13:11–12a)
   A. Knowing the time (see Luke 21:27–28)
   B. Knowing the future–salvation (see 1 Peter 1:5)
      1. When we first believed–initial, potential
      2. While we go on believing–continual, perpetual
      3. When Christ appears–final, eternal
   C. Knowing the challenge
      1. Vigilance
      2. Involvement
      3. Confidence

III. The reality of spiritual operation (Rom. 13:12b–14)
   A. Christlessness = night, darkness
   B. Christ's presence = day, light
   C. What to put off
      1. Dark deeds
      2. Indecent behavior
      3. Ill-disciplined activity
   D. What to put on
      1. Armor of light–it will be a battle
      2. Daytime decency
      3. Lord Jesus Christ–his grace and graces
   E. Control appetites

22

One Man's Faith Is Another Man's Poison

Romans 14:1-23

The church at Rome was made up of Jews and Gentiles. This was a potentially volatile mix, and Paul was concerned that the behavior of both would serve to avoid dissension and foster Christian unity.

    I. Differences of opinion are inevitable
      A. There will always be issues
        1. The "food" issue
          a. Jewish tradition
          b. Christ's teaching (Mark 7:17-19)
          c. Church's position (Acts 15:19-20)
        2. The "holy day" issue
          a. Jewish tradition
          b. Christ's practice (Matt. 12:1-14)
          c. Church's position (Col. 2:16)
      B. There will always be interpretations
        1. Jewish tendency to legalism
        2. Gentile tendency to liberty

   C. There will always be irritations
      1. The "weak" irritate the "strong" (Rom. 14:3)
      2. The "strong" irritate the "weak" (v. 1)

 II. Discernment of essentials is important (vv. 6–13)
   A. Convictions matter more than conventions
      1. People are significant
         a. In the faith–even if weakly (v. 1)
         b. God has accepted them (v. 3)
         c. Christ died for them (v. 15)
         d. They belong to the Lord (v. 8)
      2. Christ is Lord
         a. We live unto him
            (1) Eating as unto him
            (2) Abstaining as unto him
         b. We die unto him
      3. We will all appear at the *Bema* (vv. 10–11)
         a. Each will give account
         b. Each will account for himself or herself
   B. Building up is more appropriate than tearing down
      1. The place of constructive criticism
      2. The place of constructive edification

III. Discipline of attitudes is imperative (vv. 15–23)
   A. Be convinced (vv. 5, 14)
   B. Be concerned
      1. About the individual
      2. About the kingdom
   C. Be conciliatory
      1. The recognition of personal freedom
      2. The curtailing of individual rights
   D. Be considerate
      1. The "strong" consider the impact they make
      2. The "weak" consider the influence they exert

23

The Ministering Mentality

Romans 15:1-33

The desire to "please ourselves" is a powerful motivational factor. It can lead to all kinds of selfishness and inappropriate independence. Because the Christian follows Christ he or she exhibits a different attitude–the ministering mentality.

I. The ministry of edification (vv. 1–14)
   A. A matter of attitude
      1. Recognition of moral responsibility
         a. Ought (v. 1)
         b. Owe (v. 21)
         c. see Romans 1:14–15
      2. Exercise of personal restraint
         a. Sacrificial example of Christ
         b. Sacrificial restraint of self
         c. Sacrificial outreach to others
      3. Development of spiritual relationships
         a. Commitment to building up others through service
         b. Commitment to building up self through Scriptures

  B. A matter of approach (15:5-13)
    1. May the God of endurance and encouragement grant you . . .
    2. May the God of glory captivate you . . .
      a. So that his glory is a major concern
      b. So that other considerations are minor concerns
    3. May the God of peace fill you . . .
  C. A matter of application (v. 14)
    1. The willingness to accept (v. 7)
    2. The ability to cope (v. 14)

 II. The ministry of proclamation (vv. 15-21)
  A. Proclamation and penetration—"boldly"
  B. Proclamation and priesthood—"priestly duty"
  C. Proclamation and power—"Christ accomplished through me"
  D. Proclamation and purpose—"those who were not told"

 III. The ministry of administration (vv. 22-29)
  A. Completing the Corinthian ministry (v. 23)
  B. Starting the Spanish ministry (v. 24)
  C. Continuing the Roman ministry (v. 24)
  D. Finalizing the Macedonian/Achaian ministry (v. 26)
  E. Supervising the Judean ministry (v. 27)

 IV. The ministry of intercession (vv. 30-33)
  A. Intercession must be stimulated—"I urge you"
    1. By the Lord
    2. By the Spirit
  B. Intercession must be sustained—"joined in my struggle"
  C. Intercession must be specific
    1. Rescued from unbelievers
    2. Received by believers
    3. Refreshed by Romans

Thought: Where do I minister?

24

The Importance of Being Careful

Romans 16:1-27

In the first eleven chapters Paul explained the doctrine of Christianity. In the following four chapters he showed practical implications of Christian living. In the final chapter he concludes with personal greetings that are as instructive as they are illuminating. There are three things we must do.

    I. Be careful to give encouragement to people (vv. 1–16; 21–24)
       A. Receive people; e.g., Phoebe (vv. 1–2)
       B. Thank people; e.g., Priscilla and Aquila (vv. 3–5)
       C. Remember people; e.g., Epenetus (v. 5)
       D. Respect people; e.g., Andronicus, Junias (v. 7)
       E. Befriend people; e.g., Ampliatus, Stachys (vv. 8–9)
       F. Affirm people; e.g., Apelles (v. 10)
       G. Mother people; e.g., Rufus's mother (v. 13)
       H. Greet people (e.g., vv. 3–16)
          1. Note: number of women
          2. Note: number of households
          3. Note: number of house churches

  II. Be careful to give attention to problems (vv. 17–20)
    A. Be alert to destructive influences
      1. Division (v. 17)
        a. Doctrinal errors
        b. Unwarranted emphases
      2. Deception (v. 18)
        a. Pointing from Christ to self
        b. Promoting with skill and conviction
    B. Be anxious for naive believers
      1. Believers who believe anything
      2. Believers who believe everybody
    C. Be active in protective measure
      1. Watch out (v. 17)
      2. Walk away (v. 17)
      3. Wise up (v. 19)

  III. Be careful to give glory to God (vv. 25–27)
    A. Why?
      1. Because he commanded the mystery to be revealed
        a. By Christ's proclamation
        b. By Paul's gospel
        c. By prophetic teaching
      2. Because the message has universal relevance
      3. Because the gospel has eternal significance
      4. Because God alone is wise
    B. How?
      1. By obedience now
      2. Through Christ forever

Thought: After studying Romans, do I glorify God by loving obedience?

Part 2

For People on the Grow

The Epistle to the Colossians

25

How to Get Started

Colossians 1:1-8

Paul's letter to the church in Colosse was written in the customary style of his day, but it contains truth of lasting importance for people in diverse cultures in all ages. His opening greetings contain much information about the beginnings of spiritual experience.

  I. A description (v. 2a)
   A. Spiritually they were "in Christ"
   B. Morally they were "holy"
   C. Intellectually they were "believing"
   D. Sociologically they were "brothers"
   E. Geographically they were "in Colosse"

 II. An appreciation
   A. The expression of appreciation to God (v. 3)
     1. Carefully described
     2. Specifically acknowledged
   B. The evidence of the working of God
     1. Faith in Christ Jesus (v. 4)

      2. Love for all the saints (vv. 4, 8)
      3. Hope that is stored in heaven (v. 5)

III. An explanation
   A. The message
      1. God's grace in all its truth (v. 6)
      2. Gospel, which is fruitful and growing (v. 6)
      3. The word of truth, that has come to you (v. 6)
   B. The messengers
      1. Paul the apostle (v. 1; see Acts 19:9–10)
      2. Epaphras the local man (Col. 1:7)
         a. Fellow servant–*doulos*
         b. Faithful minister–*diakonos*
   C. The method (v. 7)
      1. Hearing
      2. Understanding
      3. Learning
      4. Believing
      5. Doing

26

The Search for Fulfillment

Colossians 1:9-14

It is ironic that a "growing vanguard of society perceives what Christianity calls the 'good life' to be a threat to self-fulfillment" (Carl F. H. Henry) because God made people to be fulfilled, and only he can make it happen.

I. Fulfillment through purposefulness (vv. 9–10a)
   A. The knowledge of God's will
      1. Full knowledge—*epignosis*
      2. Filled with this knowledge
      3. Applied through spiritual wisdom and understanding
   B. A life worthy of the Lord
      1. Live a life—walking
      2. Worthily—remembering your status before him
   C. Pleasing him in every way
      1. Desire to please
      2. The One to please

II. Fulfillment through fruitfulness (v. 10b)
   A. Fruitfulness as productivity
      1. External evidence of internal life
      2. Good works as evidence of true faith
   B. Fruitfulness as progress
      1. Progressive discovery of God
      2. Progressive devotion to God

III. Fulfillment through powerfulness (v. 11)
   A. The extent of power
      1. Strengthened with all power
      2. According to his glorious might
   B. The expression of power
      1. The power of endurance–response to circumstances
      2. The power of patience–restraint of self
      3. The power of joy–not stoic but Christian

IV. Fulfillment through thankfulness (vv. 12–14)
   A. Thankfulness for qualification
      1. To enjoy inheritance
      2. To be a saint in light
   B. Thankfulness for emancipation
      1. Rescue operation
      2. Dominion of darkness
   C. Thankfulness for situation
      1. Member of the kingdom
      2. King is "Son he loves"
   D. Thankfulness for redemption
      1. Freedom from sin's power
      2. Forgiveness of sin's record
      3. Remembrance of redemption's cost

V. Conclusion: If it is fulfillment that we seek, let it be found in a full understanding and acceptance of God's will, a life filled with loving devotion to Him and fully involved in doing good, all this out of a full heart.

27

King Jesus

Colossians 1:15-20

Mention of the "Kingdom of the Son" launched Paul into a magnificent description of Jesus the King. Life in the kingdom is related to appreciation of the King. Paul knew the Colossians needed to be clear on this point. So do we!

I. The magnificence of King Jesus
   A. Magnificent in the creation
      1. "Image of the invisible God" (v. 15a)
         a. Creation—man in God's image (Gen. 1:26ff.)
         b. Incarnation—Christ the image of God
         c. Regeneration—man restored (Rom. 8:29; 2 Cor. 3:18)
      2. "Firstborn over all creation" (Col. 1:15b)
         a. Not the first created being (see vv. 16-17)
         b. Firstborn—heir of all things (see Heb. 1:1-2)
      3. "By him all things were created" (Col. 1:16)
         a. "In him"—the sphere of creation
         b. "Through him"—the agent of creation
         c. "For him"—the goal of creation
      4. "He is before all things" (v. 17a)
         a. His prior existence (see John 1:1)
         b. His superior status

5. "In him all things hold together" (Col. 1:17b)
   a. He maintains and sustains
   b. He is the unifying factor
B. Magnificent in the church
   1. "The head of the body" (v. 18a)
      a. He controls
      b. He coordinates
   2. "The beginning, and firstborn from the dead" (v. 18b)
      a. Supreme conqueror of death
      b. Beginning of newness of life
      c. Risen living dynamic of the church
   3. "In everything . . . supremacy" (v. 18c)
C. Magnificent in the Christian
   1. "All his fullness dwelt in him" (v. 19)
      a. Incarnation
      b. Gnostic idea of "fullness"—totality of emanations?
      c. Christ the sole and sufficient mediator
   2. "Through him to reconcile" (v. 20a)
      a. Reconciliation
      b. God's initiative for a fallen world
      c. Christ's ministry of restoration
   3. "Through his blood . . ." (v. 20b)
      a. Redemption
      b. Harmony of all things
      c. Eventual fulfillment

II. The significance of King Jesus
A. Head of creation and church
   1. No dichotomy between material and spiritual
   2. He is Lord of "sacred" and "secular"
B. He is supreme and sufficient
   1. He creates and controls the universe
   2. So he can support and supply his people
C. He is unifying and unique
   1. We add nothing to him
   2. We keep nothing from him

28

Getting There from Here

Colossians 1:21-29

John Bunyan's famous allegory, *Pilgrim's Progress,* described the journey of the believer from the "slough of despond" to "the celestial city." In less picturesque terms Paul did the same for the Colossians. We, too, need to know how to get there from here.

    I. Where we were (v. 21)
       A. Alienated from God
       B. Antagonistic in attitude
       C. Active in evil

   II. Where we are (v. 22)
       A. We are reconciled to God
         1. Divine initiative–"He is reconciled"
         2. Divine incarnation–"Christ's physical body"
         3. Divine intervention–"through death"
       B. We are justified by God
         1. Presentation–"to present you"
           a. Holy

       b. Without blemish

       c. Free from accusation

    2. Proclamation—of justification

    3. Perseverance—"if you continue"

       a. In the faith

       b. Well founded

       c. Loyal

       d. Convinced and confident: "Continuance is the test of reality." (F. F. Bruce)

III. Where we are going (vv. 23–29)

   A. The end of our faith

     1. The hope of the gospel (v. 23)

     2. The hope of glory (v. 27)

     3. The promise of perfection (v. 28)

       a. Presentation at the *parousia*

       b. Progress of the process

   B. The means to the end

     1. Mystery as means

       a. The revelation of truth

       b. The truth of "Christ in you"

     2. Ministry as means

       a. Ministry means suffering (v. 24)

       b. Ministry means service (vv. 23, 25)

       c. Ministry means stewardship (v. 25)

       d. Ministry means sharing (v. 28)

          (1) Proclaiming

          (2) Admonishing

          (3) Teaching

             Note: "every man" (NASB) is used three times

       e. Ministry means struggling (v. 29)

29

An Ounce of Encouragement

Colossians 2:1-7

Paul's explicitly stated purpose in his ministry to the Christians in the Lycus Valley was that "they may be encouraged in heart." An ounce of encouragement, like a spoonful of sugar, goes a long way. (Note: *Parakaleo* means beseech, exhort, comfort, encourage.)

I. Encouragement inspires people (v. 1)
   A. Concern is expressed–"struggling for you"
   B. Contact is made–"all who have not met me"
   C. Communication is real–"I want you to know"
   D. Commendation is given–"I delight to see" (v. 5)

II. Encouragement instructs people (vv. 2–4)
   A. By strengthening the individual
   B. By uniting the fellowship
      1. His body
      2 The church (1:24; see Eph. 3:18)
   C. By enriching the understanding
   D. By revealing the mystery
      1. In Christ, God is made known

       2. In Christ, treasures are stored
       3. In Christ, reality is found
    E. By exposing the deceivers
       1. Test what you're taught
       2. "Nothing is so dangerous as feeble reasoning allied to fast talking." (R. C. Lucas)

III. Encouragement involves people (Col. 2:6–7)
    A. Continuing as you started
       1. You received Christ Jesus as Lord
       2. You should "walk" in him
    B. Blooming as you were planted
       1. You were rooted in him
       2. Keep in touch with your roots
    C. Developing as you were instructed
       1. You were taught correctly
       2. Progress in the faith (knowing it, doing it)
    D. Overflowing as you were enthused

30

Staying on Course

Colossians 2:8-15

Having begun their spiritual journey, the Colossians needed encouragement to continue as they had started, because factors had entered their lives that would take them off course.

    I. A word of warning (v. 8)
       A. Beware of hijackers
       B. Recognize their methods
          1. Diverting the attention
          2. Perverting the gospel
             a. Teaching that is empty and deceptive
             b. Traditions that are man made
             c. Thinking that is fundamentally "worldly"
          3. Subverting the Lord—"rather than on Christ"
       C. Resist their efforts

   II. A word of instruction (vv. 9–13)
       A. Reality of Christ
          1. In him the fullness of deity

    2. In bodily form
       a. Incarnation
       b. Crucifixion
       c. Glorification
  B. Relationship to Christ
    1. In him–"you have been given fullness"
       a. He is head
       b. You draw from him
    2. In him–"you were also circumcised"
       a. Analogy of circumcision
       b. Actuality of "Putting quite off the body of the
          flesh." (H. G. G. Moule)
    3. With him–"having been buried"
       a. Burial–termination of relationship
       b. Baptism–sign and seal of covenant and faith
    4. With him–"[you were] raised through your faith"
       a. Faith in God who raised Christ
       b. Fellowship with Christ whom God raised
    5. In him–"He forgave us"
       a. The code has been canceled
       b. The crimes have been nailed to the cross
       c. The opposition has been defeated
          (1) "Disarmed"–divested of glory, authority
          (2) "Public spectacle"–shown to be defeated
             Note: God in Christ has done all this!

III. A word of encouragement (vv. 14–15)
  A. Don't get sidetracked–by supplements to Christ
  B. Don't get hijacked–by those who diminish Christ
  C. Don't get shortchanged–by settling for less than
     Christ

31

Free to Be What?

Colossians 2:16-23

The Colossian Christians were being troubled by people who were confusing them and hindering their spiritual progress. Paul spoke forcibly to the issue, and in so doing he reminds us that we should be on our guard against those who would be less than helpful to our spiritual lives.

I. Bondage that should be avoided
   A. The bondage of legalism
      1. "What you must not do"–prohibitions on eating and drinking (v. 16a)
      2. "What you must do"–meticulous observance annually, monthly, weekly (v. 16b)
      3. Paul's rebuttal–"Don't let them judge you" (v. 17)
         a. Because they confuse shadow and substance
         b. Because they substitute ritual for reality
   B. The bondage of elitism
      1. Elitist attitudes–"delights in false humility" (v. 18a)
      2. Elitist activities–"worship of angels" (v. 18b)

3. Elitist claims—"what he has seen" (v. 18c; cf.
   2 Cor. 12:4)
4. Paul's rebuttal—"Don't let them disqualify you"
   (Col. 2:18–19)
   a. Because they are not spiritual people
   b. Because they are arrogant and empty
   c. Because they lost contact with the head
   d. Because they lost sight of the body
C. The bondage of asceticism
   1. The "dogmatics" of asceticism (v. 20)
   2. The specifics of asceticism (v. 21)
   3. Paul's rebuttal—"Why do you submit?" (v. 20)
      a. Because physical things "perish with use"
      b. Because the system is of man, not God
      c. Because there is more show than substance

II. Basics that should be remembered
   A. The basic reality of Christ
      1. In him is reality (v. 17)
      2. In him is centrality (vv. 2–3)
      3. In him is authority (v. 10)
   B. The basic reality of the church (v. 19)
      1. The controlling factor
      2. The connecting factor
      3. The coordinating factor
   C. The basic reality of the cross (v. 20)
      1. Christ died for you (vv. 13–14)
      2. You died with Christ (v. 20)
      3. Don't be dominated by what you died to (see v. 23)

III. Balance that should be maintained
   A. God's truth is found in tension
   B. Heresies solve tension by extremism
   C. Paul cautions against the latter and teaches the former
      1. Legalism is out but license is not in
      2. Elitism is out but mediocrity is not endorsed
      3. Asceticism is out but ill discipline is not acceptable

32

On Wings Like Eagles

Colossians 3:1-10

Having reminded the Colossians about the things they believe, Paul now turns his attention to how they should behave. Christians recognize that because belief and behavior are inextricably bound up in each other any erosion of belief will lead inevitably to a deterioration in behavior.

I. Set your hearts on things above (v. 1)
   A. The truth is stated
      1. Christ at God's right hand (see Ps. 110:1)
      2. Christ in whom authority resides
      3. Christ through whom audience is granted
   B. The truth is applied
      1. You have been raised with Christ
      2. Heaven is home; earth is temporary residence
      3. Eternity is reality; time is transient
   C. The truth is obeyed
      1. Set your hearts on things above
      2. Guard your affections
      3. Guide your affections
      4. Grade your affections

II. Set your minds on things above (Col. 3:2–3)
   A. The truth is stated
      1. You died–a radical termination
      2. Your life is hidden with Christ
   B. The truth is applied
      1. Life's center is Christ
      2. Life's core is hidden
   C. The truth is obeyed
      1. Set your minds on things above
      2. Divert your attention from things on earth
      3. Don't be so earthly minded you're no heavenly use

III. Put to death earthly things (vv. 4–6)
   A. The truth is stated
      1. Christ is your life
      2. Christ will appear in glory
      3. Wrath of God is coming
   B. The truth is applied
      1. Identify what is incompatible
      2. Mark what is motivational
   C. The truth is obeyed
      1. Immorality, impurity, idolatry must be dealt with
      2. The treatment must be radical

IV. Rid yourself of such things (vv. 7–10)
   A. The truth is stated
      1. You have taken off the old life
      2. You have embarked on the new life
   B. The truth is applied
      1. You used to live one way
      2. Now you are being renewed
   C. The truth is obeyed
      1. Clean up your personal life
      2. Clean up your social life

33

The View from the Pew

Colossians 3:11-17

Having reminded the Colossians about the relationship of belief and behavior in general terms, Paul now turns his attention to specifics. First, he emphasizes how Christians should behave in church.

    I. The people of the pew are people in process (v. 10)
       A. They have been redeemed
       B. They are being renewed
       C. They should be respected

   II. The people of the pew are focused on Christ (v. 11)
       A. Christ is all that matters
       B. Christ is in all his people
       C. Christ transcends the barriers
          1. Racial–Jew and Greek
          2. Religious–circumcision, uncircumcision
          3. Cultural–Greeks, Barbarians
          4. Social–slaves, freemen

III. The people of the pew are a unique community (vv. 12–14)
   A. The new church–the old Israel (see Deut. 7:6–8)
      1. Chosen
      2. Holy
      3. Loved
   B. The new character–the nature of God
      1. Christian graces–clothe yourselves . . .
      2. Christian attitudes–bear with one another
      3. Christian actions–forgive (cf. Luke 7:36ff.)
      4. Christian priority–love that binds

IV. The people of the pew are the body of Christ
   A. Individually related to Christ
   B. Collectively related to his body
      1. Governed by peace
      2. Characterized by thankfulness
      3. Permeated by the Word
      4. Enriched by praise (see Eph. 5:19)
         a. Psalms (Ps. 47:7; 1 Cor. 14:26)
         b. Hymns (Pss. 115–18; Matt. 26:30)
         c. Songs (Rev. 5:9)

V. The people of the pew are committed to glorifying God (Col. 3:17)
   A. In doing and saying what adequately represents Christ
   B. In words and deeds for which they can thank God

34

Family Living

Colossians 3:18-21

Paul continues his practical instructions by turning to the home life of the believer. He presents brief commands that he amplified in the Ephesian epistle, written about the same time.

I. Instructions to husbands and wives (vv. 18-19)
  A. Wives, submit to your husbands
    1. Submission as a normal human experience (Rom. 13:1)
    2. Submission as a particular Christian attitude
      a. To the Lord (Eph. 5:22)
      b. To each other (v. 21)
      c. To Christian leadership (1 Peter 5:5)
    3. Submission as a wife's responsibility
      a. The husband is the head (Eph. 5:23)
        (1) The one into whom we grow (4:15)
        (2) The one out of whom we grow (v. 16)
      b. The church submits to Christ (5:24)

        (1) To cooperate with his desires
        (2) To be loyal to his leadership
    4. Submission as appropriate behavior
      a. Appropriate in Colossian culture
      b. Appropriate as Christian attitude
  B. Husbands, love your wives
    1. Love as a normal human experience
    2. Love as a particular Christian attitude
      a. To the Lord (Matt. 22:37)
      b. To each other (v. 39)
    3. Love as a husband's responsibility
      a. Christ's attitude to the church (Eph. 5:25)
        (1) He gave himself up for her
        (2) He cares for and feeds her (v. 29)
        (3) He regards her as his body (v. 30)
      b. Husband's commitment to restraint
        (1) Don't be harsh
        (2) Do be kind

II. Instructions to parents and children (Col. 3: 20–21)
  A. Children, obey your parents
    1. Obedience as a normal human experience
    2. Obedience as a particular Christian attitude
      a. Man was made with a will
      b. So man is equipped with a won't
      c. Whether he will or won't determines his life
      d. Christians will to do his will (John 6:38; 7:17)
    3. Obedience as a child's responsibility
      a. Life without discipline is chaos
      b. Discipline is learned, not taught
    4. Obedience as a commendable attitude
  B. Parents, don't embitter your children (see Heb. 11:23)
    1. Beware the abuse of power
    2. Beware the misuse of privilege
    3. Beware the product of discouragement

35

In the Marketplace

Colossians 3:22-4:1

Christians are required to live on earth before they get to heaven, which means that Christianity has to be related to culture. Slavery was an integral part of first-century Greco-Roman culture, and the church had to deal with it.

I. The situation Paul confronted
   A. His Hebrew background
      1. Slavery an Old Testament fact of life (Exod. 20:10)
      2. Slavery as a partial solution (Lev. 25:35ff.)
         a. Family integration
         b. Social protection
      3. Slavery as a benevolent institution
         a. Religious privilege
         b. Guaranteed release (v. 39ff.)
   B. The Colossian situation
      1. Rome's population over 60 percent slaves
      2. Prisoners of war made slaves
      3. Rome released thousands—economic chaos
      4. Both slaves and free in congregation

II. The solution Paul offered
   A. He did not condone it
   B. He did not condemn it
   C. He did confront it
      1. In terms of status (1 Cor. 7:20–24; Gal. 3:26–28)
      2. In terms of attitude (Philem. 16–18)
      3. In terms of work ethic (Col. 3:22ff.)
         a. The key is lordship
         b. *Kyrios* = lord, master

III. The application we make
   A. A matter of masters
      1. Masters on earth (v. 22)
      2. A Master in heaven (4:1)
   B. A matter of mutuality
      1. Workers obey (3:22)
      2. Masters provide (4:1)
   C. A matter of methods
      1. Not with eye service (3:22)
      2. Not as man pleaser
   D. A matter of motivation
      1. Sincerely, not devious (v. 22)
      2. Spiritually, not materially (v. 22)
      3. Wholeheartedly, not halfheartedly (v. 23)
      4. Eternally, not temporally (vv. 24–25)
         a. Eventual reward (v. 24)
         b. Eventual repercussions (v. 25)
   E. A matter of maturity
      1. A maturity of understanding
         a. What you know (v. 24; 4:1)
         b. Who you know
      2. A maturity of application
         a. Living on earth
         b. Living for eternity

36

Keep Looking Up

Colossians 4:2-18

Paul introduced the practical section of the letter by encouraging the Colossians to "set [their] minds and hearts above." Now he concludes it with a similar instruction by reminding them of the necessity of prayer. In other words, they were to keep looking up.

I. Prayer is a dynamic
   A. It moves God to open doors (v. 3)
      1. God governs with "a degree of elasticity." (O. Hallesby)
      2. He changes circumstances (Acts 14:27)
      3. He moves people
   B. It molds people together
      1. "Pray for us" (Col. 4:3)
      2. Paul's team spirit
   C. It makes witnesses adequate (vv. 4-5)
      1. Knowing what to say
      2. Knowing how to say it
      3. Knowing how to behave

    D. It matures growing believers (v. 12)
       1. Stand firm
       2. Mature
       3. Assured

 II. Prayer is a declaration
    A. A declaration of dependence
       1. The arrogance of prayerlessness
       2. The evidence of faithfulness
    B. A declaration of delight (v. 2)
       1. The grace of thankfulness
       2. The excitement of watchfulness
    C. A declaration of devotion
       1. The majesty of Christ (3:1)
       2. The mystery of Christ (4:3)
       3. The ministry of Christ (vv. 7, 11–12)
    D. A declaration of desire
       1. The desire for enlargement (v. 3)
       2. The desire for enablement (vv. 4–6)
       3. The desire for encouragement (v. 8)
       4. The desire for establishment (v. 11)

III. Prayer is a discipline
    A. The discipline of information
       1. About the will of God (v. 12)
       2. About the circumstances of people
       3. About the world around you–"alert" (v. 2)
    B. The discipline of inspiration
       1. Prayer in the Spirit
       2. Relationship to the Spirit
    C. The discipline of perspiration
       1. Prayer as work (v. 12)
       2. Prayer as wrestling
    D. The discipline of continuation (v. 2)
       1. Faith is the geologist who finds oil
       2. Prayer is the drill that makes oil gush

Part 3

Faith with Boots On

The Epistle of James

37

Responding to Life's Testing Times

James 1:1-11

James's epistle has been the center of controversy throughout church history. Questions about authorship, date, recipients, and content abound, but on one thing there is agreement—James was essentially practical; his faith wore boots.

I. Testing times are inevitable (vv. 1–2)
   A. James's personal experience (v. 1)
      1. His brother had suffered
      2. His brethren were scattered
      3. His calling was to serve
   B. Normal Christian experience (v. 2)
      1. It is like being mugged (Luke 10:30)
      2. It is like being shipwrecked (Acts 27:41)
      3. It may be predictable, understandable, or inexplicable
      4. It is variable; e.g., poor man (James 1:9), rich man (vv. 10–11)

II. Testing times are valuable (vv. 3–4)
   A. Faith must go through fire
      1. To test its center
      2. To try its content
   B. Perseverance comes through pressure
      1. A perfecting that is progressive (see Phil. 3:12, 15)
      2. A perfecting that is productive
         a. Complete
         b. Lacking nothing

III. Testing times are manageable (James 1:2, 5–8)
   A. When we carefully consider
   B. When we continually confess
      1. We lack wisdom
      2. We need help
      3. We are totally dependent
      4. We are fully expectant
   C. When we cheerfully celebrate
      1. Joy should be evident
      2. Joy should be genuine

38

Temptation–And What to Do about It

James 1:12-21

We sometimes say facetiously that we can resist everything but temptation. But this is hardly the way to deal with a problem that is behind innumerable personal and societal ills. We need to understand temptation in order to handle it better.

I. A correct perspective on temptation
   A. It's a matter of meaning; *Peirasmos* = trial or temptation
      1. *Peirasmos* offers the opportunity to do right
      2. *Peirasmos* presents the possibility of going wrong
   B. It's a matter of blessing (v. 12)
      1. Pressure
      2. Perseverance
      3. Prospects
      4. Promise
      5. Principle

II. A clear perception of temptation
   A. Theories that must be refuted
      1. It's God's fault

      2. It's the devil who made me do it

      3. It's the woman thou gavest me

      4. It's my parents

   B. Truths that must be respected

      1. Truths about temptation (vv. 14–15)

         a. Desire

           (1) Hooked

           (2) Netted

         b. Decision

         c. Death

      2. Truths about God (vv. 13, 16–18)

         a. His character

         b. His changelessness

         c. His choice

      3. Truths about ourselves

         a. The trouble is internal

         b. Our trust is in the eternal

III. A certified prescription for temptation (vv. 19–21)

   A. Anger does not produce the life God desires, so–

      1. Be quick to listen

      2. Be slow to speak

      3. Be slow to anger

   B. Moral filth and evil are prevalent, so–

      1. Be aware of it

      2. Get rid of it

   C. The Word can save you, so–

      1. Accept it

      2. Apply it

39

The Real Thing

James 1:22-27

I. The Word must be appreciated (vv. 18, 25)
   A. Because it reveals his will—"he chose"
   B. Because it communicates his truth—"Word of truth"
   C. Because it accomplishes his purposes—"gives us birth"
   D. Because it projects his intentions—"firstfruits"
   E. Because it portrays his perfection—"perfect"
   F. Because it outlines his principles—"law"
   G. Because it offers his blessings—"liberty"

II. The Word must be accepted (vv. 21-25)
   A. This requires humility
   B. This requires receptivity—"planted in you"
      1. Well-worn path (Mark 4:15)
      2. Rocky places (vv. 16-17)
      3. Thorny ground (vv. 18-19)
      4. Good soil (v. 20)

C. This requires integrity–"Do what it says"
  1. Illustration–the man who forgot his face (James 1:23–24)
  2. Explanation
     a. Look into intently (see John 20:5)
     b. Continue in (see 1 Cor. 16:6)
     c. Not forgetting
     d. But doing
     e. This is the way of blessing (see John 13:17)

III. The Word must be applied (James 1:26–27)
  A. What man regards as satisfactory religion (v. 26)
     1. The possibility of delusion
     2. The possibility of rejection
  B. What God regards as real religion (v. 27)
     1. The place of control–"tongue"
     2. The place of compassion–"widows, orphans"
     3. The place of commitment–"world"

40

Loving Those You Don't Like

James 2:1-13

We all have our likes and dislikes, and there truly is no accounting for taste. But when our dislikes become discriminatory and prejudicial, they need correction. James is excruciatingly clear on this point.

I. A powerful exhortation (v. 1)
   A. An application of "Do what it says" (1:22)
   B. An assumption they are prone to discrimination
   C. An approach to those who "hold the faith"
      1. Lord, Lord of all—no discrimination
      2. Jesus died for all—no discrimination
      3. Christ came to all—no discrimination
      4. *Glorious*—literally, "of the glory"—he's the standard
         a. His attitude (2 Cor. 8:9)
         b. His actions (John 4:9)
   D. An appeal to evaluate attitudes and actions

II. A pointed example (James 2:2–4)
   A. An example of prejudice–external, material evaluation
   B. An example of preferential treatment–"good seat"
   C. An example of pride–"become judges"
   D. An example of pretense–cf. "discriminated" (v. 4), "doubts" (1:6)

III. A practical explanation (2:5–13)
   A. An explanation of perspective (vv. 5–7)
      1. Divine perspective (v. 5)
         a. God chooses the poor
         b. God enriches the poor
         c. God includes the poor
         d. God responds to the poor
      2. Human perspective (vv. 6–7)
         a. Insulting those God honors
         b. Pandering to the exploiters
         c. Siding with the persecutors
         d. Applauding the blasphemers
   B. An explanation of principle (vv. 8–11)
      1. The royal law applies to believers
         cf. "royal" (v. 8), "kingdom" (v. 5)
      2. The royal law forbids discrimination (v. 9)
      3. The royal law prescribes love for neighbor (v. 8)
      4. The royal law exposes sin and lawbreaking (v. 9)
   C. An explanation of priority (vv. 12–13)
      1. Mercy triumphs over judgment–see the cross
      2. Our judgment without mercy bodes ill for us
      3. We will be judged by the law of liberty
      4. The law liberates when obeyed
      5. So let's love those we don't like!

41

Show Me Your Faith

James 2:14-26

We're all familiar with the mistaken idea that it doesn't matter what you believe so long as you're sincere. James also stresses the importance of how we believe. He insists that valid faith is readily observable in action.

I. Assumptions (v. 14)
   A. People can be saved
      1. What does it mean?
      2. What does it do? (see Eph. 2:1–10)
   B. People are saved through faith
      Note: *Pistis* ("faith") occurs fifteen times in James
      1. Faith is a divine gift (v. 8)
      2. Faith appropriates divine riches (James 2:5)
      3. Faith rests in divine provision (v. 1)
      4. Faith releases divine resources (5:15)
      5. Faith endures divine testing (1:3)
   C. People need to be sure about their faith
      1. The possibility of confusion
      2. The possibility of evaluation

II. Assertions (2:15-25)
   A. Faith is dead if devoid of compassion (vv. 15-17)
      1. The condition of the underprivileged
      2. The connection between faith and love (see v. 8)
   B. Faith is more than credal confession (vv. 18-19)
      1. The danger of ritualistic repetition (see Deut. 6:4)
      2. The difference between "believing God is" and trusting God to be God
      3. Demons can recite and be awestruck
      4. But demons aren't saved
   C. Faith is shown in divine-human companionship (James 2:20-24)
      1. "Abraham believed God"—and he was credited
      2. Abraham received a call from God
      3. Abraham entered a covenant with God
      4. Abraham obeyed a command from God
      5. Abraham developed a companionship with God
         Note: "his faith was made complete . . ." (v. 22)
   D. Faith is involved in acts of courage (v. 25)
      1. Rahab had professed faith in Israel's God (see Josh. 2)
      2. Rahab had identified with God's people
      3. Rahab had accepted the consequences

III. Assimilations
   A. Does my faith express compassion?
   B. Does my faith implement confession?
   C. Does my faith involve companionship?
   D. Does my faith exhibit courage?

42

Tongue in Check

James 3:1-12

Anyone who has had a physical examination has heard the words "Put out your tongue." By looking at this peculiar organ, the doctor can tell a lot about our condition. James goes much further!

   I. The tongue needs to be considered
     A. The tool of the teacher (v. 1)
       1. A prestigious position
         Note: Rabbi = "my great one"
       2. A privileged person (Matt. 28:20; Acts 13:1)
       3. A precarious profession
         a. The teacher's tool is the tongue
         b. To whom much is given . . . (Luke 12:48)
         c. Tongues can inform and inspire or inflame and insult
     B. The measure of the mature (James 3:2–5)
       1. The tongue is slippery . . .
       2. So we all stumble . . .
       3. In the things we say . . .

    4. Therefore a disciplined tongue . . .

    5. Mirrors a mature life . . .

    6. Because the tongue is like a bit and a rudder

C. The weapon of the wicked (vv. 6–12)

    1. It is like a forest fire (v. 6)

       a. It starts in hell (Gehenna)

       b. It sparks a world of evil (appointing itself)

       c. It stains and corrupts the whole person

       d. It stays or inflames whole course of life

    2. It is like a half-tamed wild animal (vv. 7–8)

       a. Man was commissioned to control animals

       b. Man can't control himself–his tongue

       c. Restless evil is the problem (see 1:8; 3:16)

       d. Deadly poison is the result

         Note: the tongue bites sharper than the teeth

    3. It is like a polluted well (vv. 9–11)

       a. The tongue's inconsistent behavior

         (1) Constructive eulogizing of Lord and Father

         (2) Destructive traumatizing of God's creatures

       b. The tongue's unacceptable behavior

         (1) This should not be

         (2) Because wells don't give fresh and bitter water

D. The fruit of the root (v. 12)

    1. Figs grow on fig trees, not on grapevines

    2. Fruits display roots

    3. Words display hearts (Luke 6:43–45)

II. The tongue needs to be controlled

A. The problem–no man can do it

B. The principle–God changes the heart

C. The practicalities–read, mark, learn, inwardly digest

D. The prospects–continually apply (Rom. 6:11–14; Eph. 5:25–32)

E. The prayer–daily (Ps. 19:14)

43

The Good Life

James 3:13-18

The good life to which most people seem to aspire is usually related to things that will make them happy, comfortable, and troublefree. They would probably say, "The best things in life are things." James begged to differ.

  I. The good life—How do we define it?
  A. Not something we possess . . . (Luke 12:13–21)
  B. But something we express
  C. Not something glamorous . . .
  D. But something beautiful—*kalos* (see Matt. 13:45)
  E. Not something extravagant . . .
  F. But something significant—*kalos* (see 1 Tim. 4:6)

 II. The good life—How do we develop it?
  A. Application—heavenly wisdom (James 3:13)
   1. Wisdom's beginning—fear of the Lord
   2. Wisdom's blooming—understanding, "well informed"
   3. Wisdom's blessing—that which is:

    a. Pure—free from blemish
    b. Peace loving—peacemaking
    c. Considerate—yielding, gently accepting
    d. Submissive—open to reason, persuadable, persuasive
    e. Merciful—responsive to need and helplessness
    f. Impartial—beyond two-mindedness (cf. 1:6–8)
    g. Sincere—not hypocritical
  B. Attitude—humility coming from wisdom
    1. Word received with humility (1:21)
    2. Word reproducing humility
  C. Activity—deeds done in humility
    1. Sowing in peace
    2. Reaping in righteousness

III. The good life—How do we defend it?
  A. Be aware of opposite "wisdom"
    1. Not heavenly
    2. Earthly
    3. Unspiritual
    4. Devilish
  B. Be aware of contrary attitudes
    1. Bitter envy—seen in relationships (see 3:11)
    2. Selfish ambition (e.g., Phil. 1:17)
  C. Be aware of destructive activities
    1. Producing chaotic disorder (see James 1:8)
    2. Producing evil practice—mean, worthless behavior

44

Trouble and Strife

James 4:1-10

"Peacemakers who sow in peace raise a harvest of righteousness," says James. But he is practical enough to know that trouble and strife are all too common and they need to be addressed.

I. Admit the problem (vv. 1–2)
   A. Relational tensions are all too common
      1. Fighting–literally "wars"
      2. Quarreling–literally "fights"; metaphorically, see 2 Timothy 2:23–24
      3. Killing (see Matt. 5:21, 24)
         Note: applicable across relational spectrum
   B. Diversionary tactics are all too easy
      1. Denying the tension
      2. Disregarding the tension
   C. Creative treatments are all too rare
      1. Admitting a problem exists
      2. Approaching the issue with care
      3. Asking the questions that will help–"What causes . . . ?"

II. Analyze the problem
   A. The "pleasure" problem (James 4:2a)
      1. "Desires," "wants," "covet"–morally neutral
      2. But, "desires battle within you"–internal concern; "desires battle among you"–relational conflict
      3. But, "wants"–internal reaction
      4. But, "covet" is denied–inner strife
        "It is at root no more than the existence in each of us of a self-centred heart, a controlling spirit of self interest." (Motyer)
   B. The "prayer" problem (vv. 2b–3)
      1. Prayerlessness–getting by self-effort, self-assertion
      2. Inappropriate prayer–using God to foster self-interest
      3. Unanswered prayer–leading to frustration, resentment
   C. The "priority" problem (vv. 4–5a)
      1. The antagonism of "God" and "world"
      2. The exclusiveness of "friend" and "enemy"
      3. The conflict of "Spirit" and "selfishness"
   D. The "pride" problem (vv. 5b–6)
      1. Pride fills you with yourself
      2. Humility fills you with grace

III. Address the problem (vv. 7–10)
   A. A provision–more grace
   B. A program–more obedience
      1. Submit–not surrender but enlistment
      2. Resist–not blue skies but conflict
      3. Draw near–not isolation but communion
      4. Clean hands–clean up your act
      5. Purify hearts–reorientate and refocus
      6. Grieve
      7. Mourn
      8. Wail–genuine repentance
      9. Change attitude–trade self-centered pleasure for serious commitment
     10. Humble yourselves–and he will uplift

45

Curbing Criticism and Cockiness

James 4:11-17

J ames insists that the problems Christians experience are often caused by attitudes that are wrong. His solution is "humble yourselves before the Lord. . . ." Criticism and cockiness aren't evidences of humility and must be curbed.

I. Curbing the critical spirit (vv. 11–12)
   A. What do we mean by a critical spirit?
      1. What it isn't
         a. Judicial activity (Acts 4:19–20)
         b. Careful analysis (John 7:24)
         c. Spiritual oversight (Gal. 6:1; 1 John 4:1)
         d. Personal evaluation (1 Cor. 4:3; 11:31–32)
      2. What it is
         a. *Katalaleite*–talking against, behind, down
         b. Example of Miriam and Aaron (Num. 12:1–16)
   B. What is so wrong about a critical spirit?
      1. It destroys relationships–"brother," "neighbor"
      2. It disregards the law–"speaks against the Law"

3. It defies God—"only one Judge . . ."
   Note: James 2:13
4. It deludes us—"Who are you?" (see Matt. 7:1–5)
C. What do we do about it?
   1. Recognize it
   2. Repudiate it
   3. Repent of it
   4. "Humble ourselves"

II. Curing the cocky attitude (James 4:13–17)
   A. What do we mean by a cocky attitude?
      1. "I have all the time in the world"—"today, tomorrow"
      2. "I can go anywhere I wish"—"this or that city"
      3. "I'll do my own thing"—"carry on business"
      4. "I'll make myself a bundle"—"and make money"
   B. What's so wrong about a cocky attitude?
      1. It denies limitations (v. 13)
         a. Of knowledge—"you don't know"
         b. Of control—"what will happen"
         c. Of ability—"boast and brag"
      2. It ducks issues (v. 14)
         a. Issue of meaning
         b. Issue of frailty
         c. Issue of transience
         d. Issue of significance
   C. What do we do about it? (vv. 15–16)
      1. We must acknowledge that
         a. All planning is done in light of Providence
         b. All boasting is dangerously close to blasphemy
      2. We must act:
         a. Because to know and not to do is sin
         b. Because to know and not to do is stupid

46

Imminent Return–Immediate Concern

James 5:1-12

The return of Christ in glory, or the second advent, will be in marked contrast to his initial coming, or first advent, in obscurity and humility. People look at this facet of Christian doctrine differently, but James, true to form, views it practically and outlines the concern that accompanies an understanding of the return.

I. The imminent return of Christ
   A. The promise is certain
      1. The Savior's teaching (see Matt. 24:27, 37, 39, 42, 44)
      2. The Master's assurance (John 14:3)
      3. The angels' affirmation (Acts 1:11)
      4. The apostles' proclamation (1 Thess. 4:15–16)
   B. The program is concealed
      1. Pre-, post-, or amillenialism?
      2. The timing is not advertised (Matt. 24:42–51)
   C. The practicalities are compelling

1. It is the Lord who is coming—so acknowledge him (James 5:7)
2. His coming is near—so await him (v. 8)
3. He will judge in righteousness—so obey him (v. 9)
4. He will bring things to completion (*telos*)—so trust him (v. 11)

II. The immediate concern of Christians
   A. Concern about prosperity (vv. 1–6)
      1. Prosperity as prize—capitalist, communist dogma
      2. Prosperity as problem (Matt. 6:24; 1 Tim. 6:10)
         a. Hoarding (James 5: 2–3; see Matt. 6:19–21)
            (1) Grain (rotting)
            (2) Clothes (moth-eaten)
            (3) Precious metals (rusting)
         b. Cheating (James 5:4)
            (1) People matter more than prosperity (see Isa. 5:9ff.)
            (2) Principle more significant than prosperity
               Note: "Lord Almighty"
         c. Indulging (James 5:5)
            (1) The ill discipline of excessive consumption
            (2) The shortsightedness of selfish indulgence
         d. Abusing (v. 6)
            (1) Beating the defenseless
            (2) Capitalizing on the underprivileged
               Note: What is prosperity doing to me? What am I doing with prosperity?
   B. Concern about patience (vv. 7–12)
      1. Explanation
         a. Patience—under stress (vv. 7–9)
            (1) Patience bears its own fruit
            (2) Impatience receives its own condemnation
         b. Stand firm—under pressure (cf. Luke 9:51)
         c. Persevere—under suffering (James 5:10–11)
            (1) Perseverance wins respect

          (2) Perseverance brings joy
          (3) Perseverance assures completion
  2. Example–Job, prophets
  3. Exhortation (v. 12)
     a. Say what you mean, mean what you say
     b. If you promise, follow through
     c. Integrity is mandatory; anything else will be judged

47

Prayer and Healing

James 5:13-18

Having advocated patience and perseverance, James instructed his readers concerning what they should do while being patient. Among other things, they should pray. Let's look at what he meant by prayer and what it accomplishes.

I. The dynamic force of prayer (v. 16)
   A. Prayer is a potent power (see Matt. 5:13; 9:12; 1 Peter 4:11)
   B. Prayer packs a punch (see Eph. 3:20; Col. 1:29)
   C. Prayer is a precious privilege–"righteous man"
      1. Not perfect but forgiven
      2. Not superman but "like us"; e.g., Elijah (1 Kings 17–19)
         a. Dynamic then depressed
         b. Courageous then cowardly
         c. Motivated then maudlin
      3. Not superb intelligence but supernatural intervention

II. The decisive factors of prayer
   A. The obedience factor–prayer is mandated
   B. The faith factor (James 5:15)
      1. "Name it and claim it?"–faith as expectancy

      2. Prayer for guidance, prayer for faith?–faith as belief
      3. Prayer based on "Thy will be done"?–faith as rest, trust
    C. The sovereignty factor
      Note: 1:5–8; 4:2–3
      1. The name of the Lord (5:14)
      2. The Lord will raise him (v. 15)

III. The different forms of prayer
    A. The prayer of the individual at all times (v. 13)
      1. In times of consternation–prayer
      2. In times of celebration–praise
    B. The prayer of the elders in times of sickness (vv. 14–15)
      1. The request of the sick person
        a. Not trivial?
        b. Not terminal?
      2. The response of the elders
        a. Pray in the name of the Lord
        b. Anoint in the name of the Lord
          (1) Symbolic
          (2) Sacramental
          (3) Medicinal
      3. The results of the prayer/anointing
        a. Made well
        b. Raised up
        c. Sins forgiven
          Note: "If" (Mark 2:1–12; John 9:1–3; 1 Cor. 11:30); also note: Timothy (1 Tim. 5:23), Trophimus (2 Tim. 4:20), Paul (2 Cor. 12:7–10)
    C. The prayer of believers in times of estrangement (James 5:16)
      1. Sin against each other
      2. Confess to one another
      3. Pray with each other
      4. Healing for each other

48

Bringing the Wanderers Home

James 5:19-20

James has spoken about those who are in trouble, those who are happy, those who are sick, and those who are having relational problems, and he has explained what should be done. But what about those who are wandering away? What should be done about them?

    I. We should wonder as they wander
       A. Wondering about their condition
          1. Are they unbelievers who fooled us?
          2. Are they unbelievers who fooled themselves?
          3. Are they believers who are backsliding?
          4. Are they believers who are apostatizing?
       B. Wondering about the causes
          1. Influence of seductive agencies (2 Peter 2:15)
          2. Ignorance of scriptural truth (Mark 12:24–27)
             a. The truth and regeneration (James 1:16–18)
             b. The truth and liberation (John 8:32)
             c. The truth and obligation (Gal. 5:7)
             d. The truth and motivation (1 John 3:18–19)
          3. Insistence on self-deception (1:8)

II. We should worry as they wander
   A. The issue of a life lived in error
      1. Getting off on the wrong foot
      2. Heading off in the wrong direction
      3. Building on the wrong advice
      4. Teaming up with the wrong people
      5. Finishing up in the wrong place
   B. The issue of the death of a soul
      1. There's more to a man than body (Matt. 10:28)
      2. There's more to life than success (16:26)
      3. There's more to reality than here and now
   C. The issue of a multitude of sins
      1. The variety of sins
      2. The enormity of guilt
      3. The immensity of need

III. We should work as they wander
   A. The privilege of this work
      1. Only God can do it
      2. But he chooses to use people
   B. The principles of this work
      1. Bringing back
      2. Turning
      3. Saving
      4. Covering
   C. The priorities of this work
      1. If they wander like sheep . . .
      2. The Shepherd goes after them (see 18:12; 1 Peter 2:25)
   D. The practicalities of this work
      1. Intercession
      2. Initiative
      3. Involvement

Part 4

When the Going Gets Tough

The First Epistle of Peter

49

Knowing What to Read

I Peter 1:1-2

At some time in the early to mid 60s A.D., the Christians in Rome were persecuted. Peter, sensing that things were going to get worse, wrote this letter of instruction and encouragement to believers scattered around the empire.

I. The significance of the epistle (v. 1)
   A. The writer
      1. A changed man who exhibited authenticity— "Thou art . . . thou shalt be" (John 1:42)
      2. A called man who exuded authority—apostle, foundation (Eph. 2:20)
      3. A convinced man who expressed ability
         a. Conviction in testimony (Matt. 16:13–17)
         b. Conviction in proclamation (Acts 2:36)
   B. The recipients
      1. Special to God—"elect"
         a. Israel the chosen people (Isa. 43:20–21)
         b. Church the chosen community (Gal. 6:16)

    2. Strangers to world
      a. The example of Abraham (Heb. 11:8–13)
      b. The experience of Christians (13:13–14)
    3. Scattered to serve–"Diaspora"
      a. The breadth of base
      b. The spread of truth

  II. The scope of the epistle (1 Peter 1:2a)
    A. The explanation of salvation
      1. The work of the Father
        a. Choosing to reveal himself as Father
        b. Choosing to redeem his people as children
      2. The work of the Son
        a. The shedding of his blood
        b. The sprinkling of his blood (see Exod. 24:3–8; Heb. 9:12–14; 10:19–22)
      3. The work of the Spirit
        a. Sanctification–an accomplished fact (1 Cor. 6:11)
        b. Sanctification–a progressive necessity (2 Cor. 3:16–18)
    B. The application of salvation
      1. The call to obedience
      2. The essence of lordship
      3. The nature of discipleship

 III. The strength of the epistle (1 Peter 1:2b)
    A. Multiplied grace for monumental problems
    B. Multiplied peace in horrendous situations

50

A Positive Attitude

1 Peter 1:3-5

Peter, living in the midst of trying circumstances with grave misgiving about the future, was able to maintain a positive attitude and encourage others to do likewise.

I. Desiring a positive attitude
   A. The tendency to negative attitudes (e.g. Mark 14:66–72)
      1. The enormity of the problem
      2. The difficulty of the solution
      3. The tendency to capitulate
   B. The necessity of positive attitudes
      1. In order to live as we ought
      2. In order to glorify God as we should
      3. In order to function as we desire

II. Developing a positive attitude
   A. The basic–a solid grasp of truth
      1. A gift of a new birth (1 Peter 1:3)
         a. A gift of great mercy

   b. A gift of living hope
   c. A gift of boundless certainty
  2. The gift of a new status (v. 4)
   a. Heirs of an inheritance (cf. Matt. 6:19–21;
    Luke 12:13–21)
   b. An incorruptible inheritance–*aphthartos*
   c. An undefiled inheritance–*amiantos*
   d. An unfading inheritance–*amarantos*
   e. An unassailable inheritance (e.g., Acts
    12:4–6)
  3. The gift of a new security (1 Peter 1:5)
   a. Guarded by God's power (e.g., 2 Cor. 11:32)
   b. Guarded through man's faith
   c. Guarded unto salvation
 B. The building–a steady application of truth
  1. Through constant study
  2. Through constant reminder
  3. Through constant encouragement

III. Demonstrating a positive attitude
 A. The demonstration of praise (1 Peter 1:3)
  1. Praise that is spontaneous
  2. Praise that is intelligent
 B. The demonstration of hope (e.g., vv. 13, 21)
  1. Hope that is expectant
  2. Hope that is persistent
 C. The demonstration of faith
  1. Faith that is well grounded
  2. Faith that is well nurtured

51

Joy-Filled Living

1 Peter 1:6-9

Many people find the pursuit of happiness as frustrating as it is tiring. Joy is a Christian distinctive that even those who are experiencing difficulties may enjoy.

   I. The joy that comes through faith
      A. The ground of faith (v. 6)
         1. The revelation of the Father's mercy
         2. The result of the Son's ministry
         3. The reality of the Spirit's presence
            Note: "in this" relates to vv. 1–5
      B. The growth of faith (vv. 6b–7)
         1. Growth in value–"greater than gold"
         2. Growth in validity–"proved genuine"
         3. Growth in valor–"all kinds of trials"
      C. The goal of faith (vv. 7b–8)
         1. Now we believe without seeing

       2. Then we will see what we believed; e.g., the experience of Thomas (John 20:24–30)

  II. The joy that comes through hope
     A. The hope of comparison
       1. "The little while" and "the last time"
       2. "The grief I suffer" and "the blood he shed"
       3. "The gold that perishes" and "the inheritance that remains"
     B. The hope of completion
       1. The certainty of Christ's return (1 Peter 1:7b)
       2. The assurance of salvation's results (v. 9)

 III. The joy that comes through love (v. 8)
     A. The joy of loving
       1. Love's commitment (John 18:10)
       2. Love's communion (21:15)
       3. Love's communication (vv. 20–22)
     B. The joy of being loved
       1. We love him because he loved us
       2. We accept him because he accepts us

52

Taking Salvation Seriously

I Peter 1:10-12

Peter, because of his circumstances, was particularly concerned that his attention should be focused on lasting values, and he wanted to ensure that other believers would take their salvation seriously. This is a prime need today.

I. The curse of casualness
   Note: this casualness can be on an institutional or individual level
   A. The casualness of disbelief
   B. The casualness of disinterest
   C. The casualness of disdain

II. The strength of seriousness
   A. Seriousness and a sense of privilege
      1. The intensity of the prophets' search (v. 10)
         a. The limits of their revelation; e.g., Simeon (Luke 2:25)
         b. The uncertainty of their illumination; e.g., John (Matt. 11:3)

    2. The eagerness of the angel's interest (1 Peter 1:12)
      a. The scope of their knowledge
      b. The limit of their experience
    3. The flow of the missionary endeavor (v. 12)
      a. The arrival of the early missionaries
      b. The interest of the embattled apostle
B. Seriousness and a sense of authenticity
    1. Spirit inspired prophecy
      a. Peter's understanding of inspiration (2 Peter 1:19–21)
      b. Peter's use of prophecy (Acts 1:20; 2:14–21, 25–28, 34–35)
    2. Spirit inspired preaching
      a. Spirit inspired Scripture (2 Tim. 3:16)
      b. Spirit inspired speakers (Acts 1:8)
      c. Spirit inspired response (10:44)
C. Seriousness and a sense of wonder
    1. The wonder of divine grace (1 Peter 1:10)
    2. The wonder of Christ's sufferings (v. 11)
      a. Clearly predicted (Mark 14:27)
      b. Personally witnessed (v. 33)
    3. The wonder of promised glories (1 Peter 1:11)
      a. The glorious resurrection (Acts 2:27)
      b. The glorious ascension (1:9–11)
      c. The glorious kingdom (4:11)
D. Seriousness and a sense of timing
    1. Previous eras pointed to our era (1 Peter 1:12)
    2. Present circumstances point to serious situations

III. Calculated carefulness
   A. Carefulness about your own spiritual position
   B. Carefulness about your own spiritual condition
   C. Carefulness about your own spiritual expression

53

Be Holy

1 Peter 1:13-16

All the ethical demands of God upon his people can be summarized in the call to "Be holy." Despite its obvious simplicity, this command has been greeted with great confusion, neglect, and apprehension by believers and derision by unbelievers. Nevertheless, the word is still operative: "Be holy because I am holy."

I. Holiness defined
   A. Original meaning—"separation" or "cutting off"
   B. Special meaning—God's autobiographical description, "I am holy . . ." (Josh. 24:19; Ps. 99:3; Isa. 6:1–3)
   C. Practical meaning—people and things set apart for God; e.g., Sabbath (Gen. 2:3; Exod. 20:8–11)
   D. Ethical meaning; e.g., Old Testament development from ceremonial to ethical (Lev. 19); New Testament development of internal from external (1 Peter 1:2)

II. Holiness desired
   A. Factors that motivate towards holiness

    1. The character of God—"Be holy because I am"
    2. The call of God—"he who called you is holy"
    3. The command of God
    4. The consistency of God—"it is written . . ."
    5. The choice of God—"therefore"
 B. Factors that militate against holiness
    1. The devil who rebelled against the Father
    2. The world that crucified the Son
    3. The flesh that lusts against the Spirit

III. Holiness developed
 A. The divine ingredient—the ministry of the Holy Spirit (v. 2)
 B. The human ingredients
    1. A well-ordered mind (v. 13)
     a. The tragedy of an unenlightened mind
     b. The waste of an untidy mind
     c. The shame of an unexercised mind
    2. A well-disciplined life (v. 13)—"sober"
     a. The identification of limits
     b. The appreciation of limits
     c. The application of limits
    3. A well-defined goal (v. 13)—"set your hope"
     a. "Grace" the basis of hope
     b. "Christ" the means of hope
     c. "Appearing" the realization of hope
    4. A well-established conversion (v. 14)—"do not conform"
     a. A change of status—"children of obedience"
     b. A change of understanding—"you lived in ignorance"
     c. A change of desire—"the evil desires you had"

54

A Sense of Values

1 Peter 1:17-25

Surrounded by the might and glory of the Roman Empire and threatened by the rage and fury of the emperor, Peter and his fellow believers might have been intimidated. The apostle, however, gets everything in perspective by outlining some basic values.

I. Things that must be underlined
   A. External appearances are deceptive (v. 17)
      1. "Impartiality" related to "prosperous" = "mask"
      2. Peter's hard lesson in Caesarea (Acts 10:34)
   B. Financial resources are perishable (1 Peter 1:18a)
      1. Fluctuating real value
      2. Negligible redemptive value (cf. Matt. 6:19ff.)
   C. Traditional norms are suspect (1 Peter 1:18b)
      1. The forefathers were not infallible
      2. Time substitutes ritual for reality (cf. John 7:37)
   D. Temporal issues are transient (1 Peter 1:20)
      1. Life is part of the creation
      2. Today is part of the "last times"

  E. Spiritual experiences are confusing (v. 23)
    1. The possibilities of pseudoregeneration
    2. The proliferation of misinformation
  F. Mortal men are finite (v. 24a)
    1. The grass may be significant
    2. The grass is still grass
  G. Cultural glories are ephemeral (v. 24a)
    1. The message of prophecy
    2. The evidence of history

 II. Truths that must be understood
  A. The Fatherhood of God
    1. The Father who judges impartially (v. 17)
    2. The Father who hears compassionately (v. 17)
    3. The Father who redeemed eternally (v. 19)
    4. The Father who planned sovereignly (v. 20)
    5. The Father who triumphed gloriously (v. 21)
  B. The saviorhood of Christ
    1. The sacrificial aspect (v. 19a)
    2. The substitutionary aspect (v. 19b)
    3. The saving aspect (v. 18)
      "redeemed"–"to release by paying a ransom"
  C. The brotherhood of believers
    1. We appeal to the same Father
    2. We are born of the same seed
    3. We obey the same truth
    4. We share the same love

 III. Tasks that must be undertaken
  A. The development of a reverent lifestyle
  B. The development of a confident attitude
  C. The development of a fervent relationship

55

Spiritual Growth

1 Peter 2:1-3

If it is true that when the going gets tough the tough get going, Christians need to recognize the need for spiritual toughness in their confrontation of spiritual tough situations. Peter calls it "growing up in your salvation."

I. The initiation of spiritual growth
    A. The proclamation of the Word (1:25)
        1. The living Word
        2. The enduring Word
        3. The Word of truth
    B. The introduction to the Son of God (v. 3)
        1. The invitation to "taste and see" (Ps. 34:8)
        2. To experience that "the Lord is good"
    C. The reception of the life of God (1 Peter 1:3-4, 23)
        1. The reality of this new life
        2. The possibilities of this new life
    D. The recognition of the people of God (v. 22)
        1. The infant in the family
        2. The adults in the family

II. The stimulation of spiritual growth (v. 2)
Note: "sincere milk of the word" or "pure milk"–
logikos from *logos* = "word," "reason," or "spirit"
   A. The appetite created by hearing the Word of God
   B. The appetite created by knowing the Son of God
   C. The appetite created by experiencing the life of God
   D. The appetite created by relating to the people of God
   E. The appetite created by discovering the salvation of God

III. The consolidation of spiritual growth (v. 1)
   A. Recognition of behavior
      1. Through the Word of God (Matt. 16:23)
      2. Through the example of Christ (Luke 5:8)
      3. Through the confrontation of believers (Gal. 2:11)
   B. Repentance for behavior
      1. Calling sin sin
      2. Changing attitude toward sin
   C. Rejection of behavior
      1. Rejection of malice
         a. Analyze the desire to harm
         b. Accept the opportunity to help
      2. Rejection of guile
         a. Identify the desire to deceive
         b. Embark on the path to honesty
      3. Rejection of hypocrisy
         a. Admit the tendency to conceal
         b. Accept the necessity to confess
      4. Rejection of envy
         a. Recognize the resentment of the other person
         b. Concentrate on the development of own resources
      5. Rejection of slander
         a. Be aware of what is fair, true, and necessary
         b. Be concerned about building up not tearing down

56

Building on the Rock

1 Peter 2:4-8

Peter (Greek *Petros*) was called the rock (Greek *petra*) on which Christ would build his church, but Peter called Christ "the living stone" and "the rock" and said that all believers, like living stones, are built up in Christ. When the going gets tough, what and how and where you are building is important.

I. Christ–the living stone
   A. The divine revelation of the living stone
      1. Prophetic pronouncement
         a. Jehovah's promise of judgment (Isa. 8:12ff.)
         b. Jehovah's principle of justice (Isa. 28:16ff.)
         c. Jewish psalm of jubilation (Ps. 118:22)
      2. Messianic parable (Mark 11:1-2)
         a. The vineyard
         b. The violence
         c. The vindication
      3. Apostolic preaching (Acts 4:1-12)
         a. The rejected stone–Christ crucified

   b. The capstone–Christ exalted
   c. The cornerstone–Christ established
   d. The living stone–Christ appropriated (John 7:27)
   e. The stumbling stone–Christ rejected
B. The human reaction to the living stone
   1. The God-given freedom to react
   2. The God-ordained consequences of reaction (1 Peter 2:8b)
      a. The stone will become a mountain (Dan. 2:31ff.)
      b. Those who respond will be secure (1 Peter 2:6)
      c. Those who reject will stumble (v. 8a)

II. Christians–the living stones
   A. Establishing the relationship with him
      1. Admit
      2. Believe
      3. Come
      4. Discover
   B. Developing the relationship with him
      1. Living like a living stone
      2. Growing into a spiritual house
      3. Sharing in a holy priesthood
      4. Participating in a spiritual sacrifice

57

The Pressures of Privilege

1 Peter 2:9–12

Peter explains to the believers that they are a specially privileged group of people. When understood this should give them great confidence in facing the future, but it also puts the pressure of privilege upon them.

I. The place of privilege (see also Exod. 19:1–6; Isa. 43:19–21)
  A. The privilege of becoming "a people" (1 Peter 2:9–10)
    1. A chosen people
       a. Chosen to be a people
       b. "We the people . . ."
    2. A holy people
       a. Distinctive in identity
       b. Distinguished by purity
    3. A special people
       a. Specially purchased
       b. Prize possession (e.g., Mal. 3:17)
    4. A called people
       a. The former state of darkness
       b. The present state of light

       5. A pitied people
         a. A state of helplessness (e.g., Mark 10:47)
         b. An attitude of compassion
    B. The privilege of being "a priesthood"
       1. The privilege of immediate access
       2. The promise of eternal kingdom

II. The price of privilege
    A. Accepting the status (1 Peter 2:11)
       1. A declaration of difference
       2. A degree of detachment
    B. Abstaining from seduction (v. 11)
       1. Natural passions contrary to spiritual well-being
       2. Spiritual principle conquering natural passion
    C. Absorbing the slander (v. 12)
       1. "Atheism, Thyestian feasts, Oedipodean inter-
          course" (Athenagoras)
       2. Standing secure in the truth
       3. Anticipating the final tribunal

III. The practice of privilege
    A. Declare the virtues of the God above you—"Declare
       the praises" = "Publish abroad the virtues"
    B. Decline the vices of the society around you—"Live
       good lives among the pagans"
    C. Define the values of the world against you
       1. Stand for what is eternally good
       2. Live for what will glorify God

58

The Christian Citizen

1 Peter 2:13-17

The Christian life is lived in the secular world under the scrutiny of God and man. In order that God might be honored and man challenged, certain standards of behavior are expected, particularly in the area of citizenship. Peter specifies three things: authority, liberty, and dignity.

I. Authority and the Christian citizen
   A. The Christian citizen's recognition of authority
      1. Authority in principle
         a. God's character assumes it
         b. God's creation requires it
         c. God's children need it
      2. Authority in practice
         a. Authorities have been instituted (v. 13; see Rom. 13:1)
         b. Responsibilities have been indicated (1 Peter 2:14)
   B. The Christian citizen's response to authority
      1. Submission because it is enjoined by God (v. 13)

  2. Submission because it is ingrained by the Spirit
     (1:14)
  3. Submission because it is enacted by Christ
  4. Insubordination when it contravenes God's authority (Acts 5:29)

II. Liberty and the Christian citizen
   A. The experience of liberty
      1. The law of liberty in terms of definition (James
         1:25)
      2. The limits of liberty in terms of dependence
      3. The life of liberty in terms of discipleship (1 Peter
         2:16c)
   B. The excesses of liberty (v. 16b)
      1. Liberty as a cloak for license
      2. Liberty as an excuse for laziness
      3. Liberty as a rationale for lawlessness
   C. The exercise of liberty (v. 16a; see Acts 12:1ff.)
      1. Freely choose the life of service
      2. Clearly show the acts of submission

III. Dignity and the Christian citizen
   A. The Christian approach to dignity (1 Peter 2:17)
      1. The dignity of the individual as created by God
      2. The dignity of the brotherhood as purchased by
         God
      3. The dignity of the Lord revealed as God
      4. The dignity of the king as ordained by God
   B. The Christian affirmation of dignity
      1. Respect in mortal matters
      2. Love in ecclesiastical matters
      3. Reverence in spiritual matters
      4. Cooperation in societal matters

IV. Remember—this is called "doing good," and it muzzles
    the critics!

59

Injustice

1 Peter 2:18-25

Injustice has never been more clearly expressed than in the institution of slavery. The early church's approach to the problem is enlightening, and Peter's instruction to slaves contains principles of behavior for Christians who suffer injustice in all ages.

I. Injustice and the extreme of slavery
   A. Slavery and the pagan world
      1. The treatment of persons as property
      2. "Masters and slaves have nothing in common, a slave is a living tool." (Aristotle)
      3. The source of slaves
         a. Born slaves
         b. Captured slaves
         c. Self-sold
         d. Bankruptcy
         e. Traded slaves
      4. The release of slaves was regulated
      5. The treatment of slaves varied (v. 18)
   B. Slavery and the biblical world
      1. The relatively humane aspects of Old Testament teaching (Lev. 25:44ff.)
      2. The economic structure of New Testament times

      3. The slave viewed as spiritual person (cf. 1 Peter 2:5, 18)

      4. The slave and master in Christian fellowship (v. 16)

      5. The slave as submissive witness (v. 18)

II. Injustice and the example of the Savior
   A. The injustice of his trials (Mark 14:53–15:20)
      1. Irregularities in the proceedings
      2. Innocence confirmed by the judge
      3. Implacability of his accusers
   B. The inhumanity of his cross (15:21–41)
      1. The calculated shame of crucifixion
      2. The undisguised hostility of the crowds
      3. The vilification of the thieves
      4. The desertion of the disciples
      5. The separation from the Father
   C. The importance of his example
      1. Entrusting to God's hands rather than his own (1 Peter 2:23)
      2. Enduring on behalf of those he understood (v. 21)
      3. Enriching with healing those who were wounded (v. 24)

III. Injustice and the experience of the shepherd
   A. Recognizing the root of injustice
      1. The rejection of divine standards
      2. The preference for individual standards
   B. Returning to the shepherd (v. 25)
      1. Admitting our own waywardness
      2. Accepting his watchcare (overseer = *episkopos*)
   C. Responding to the call (v. 21)
      1. The call to uniqueness
      2. The challenge to submissiveness
   D. Relating to the cross (v. 24)
      1. We died, in him, to sin
      2. We live, through him, unto righteousness

60

Marriage in Focus

1 Peter 3:1-7

The emphasis on the importance of relationships continues with this passage on marriage. The divine institution of marriage is always open to attack, but it is a great resource in tough times.

I. Applying the principles of Christian marriage (v. 7)
   A. Applying the principle of spiritual equality
      1. Seeing you are heirs together
         a. Of grace
         b. Of life
      2. Saying your prayers together
         a. Evidence of attitude
         b. Indication of gratitude
      3. Sharing your cares together
         a. An automatic recourse
         b. An agreed resource
   B. Applying the principle of sexual mutuality
      Note: *Sunoikein* = to live together
      1. Marriage–an exercise in mutuality
         a. Mutual comfort
         b. Mutual companionship

          c. Mutual completion
      2. Consummation—an exercise in consideration
          a. Caring for each other
          b. Communicating with each other
   C. Applying the principle of physical disparity
      Note: "the weaker partner" is purely physical
      1. Sensitivity to physical limitations
      2. Adaptability to emotional pressures (see Matt. 19:27–30; 1 Cor. 9:5)
   D. Applying the principle of practical authority (1 Peter 3:1)
      1. The equality of male and female
      2. The authority of male over female
      3. The responsibility of female to male

II. Approaching the problem of mixed marriage (vv. 1–6)
   A. Mixed marriage is expressly forbidden (2 Cor. 6:14–16)
   B. Mixed marriage is perfectly possible
      1. The unbelief of the husband
      2. The undertaking of the wife
   C. Mixed marriage is carefully handled
      1. Careful attention to behavior
          a. Practicing quietness, not picking quarrels
          b. Learning cooperation, not loving confrontation
          c. Highly visible, not horribly vocal
      2. Careful attention to beauty
          a. Expressive character, not expensive clothes
          b. Inner attitude, not outer adornment
      3. Careful attention to bravery (1 Peter 3:6)
          a. The courage not to panic
          b. The consistency not to compromise

III. Appreciating the privilege of demonstrating marriage
   A. This is of great worth in God's sight (v. 4)
   B. This is of great value in pagan society (2:12)

61

Loving Life

1 Peter 3:8-12

It is interesting to note that Peter does not encourage the believers to work towards survival but rather to live life in such a way that even in tough times they will love it.

I. The place of belief
   A. Belief about the existence of the Lord (v. 12)
      1. The Lord of reality
      2. The Lord of righteousness
      3. The Lord of relationship
   B. Belief about the experience of life (v. 10)
      1. Life that must be endured (Eccles. 2:17)
      2. Life that may be enjoyed
   C. Belief about the exercise of liberty (1 Peter 3:11)
      1. Liberty to discern
      2. Liberty to desire
      3. Liberty to decide

II. The place of behavior
   A. Behavior as it relates to convictions

B. Behavior as it relates to circumstances
    1. Circumstances that are basically agreeable (v. 8)
    2. Circumstances that are thoroughly disagreeable (v. 9)
C. Behavior as it relates to choices
    1. Choices related to "mind-set" (e.g., Mark 8:33)
    2. Choices related to "suffering together" (e.g., Acts 3:1–10)
    3. Choices related to "loving as brothers" (e.g., 4:23)
    4. Choices related to "inner feelings" (e.g., 1 John 3:17)
    5. Choices related to "lowly minded" (e.g., 1 Peter 5:5)
D. Behavior as it relates to calling (3:9)
    1. Called not to react naturally
    2. Called to respond supernaturally

III. The place of blessing
  A. The concept of blessing
    1. To "speak well of"
    2. To "think well of"
  B. The consciousness of blessing
    1. The sense of divine approval
    2. The security of divine involvement
  C. The conditions of blessing
    1. The consistency of God's position
    2. The certainty of God's blessing

62

What Really Matters?

1 Peter 3:13-16

Sometimes when things get difficult, judgment is impaired, principles are abandoned, and serious mistakes are made. In preparation for tough times, wise people have already decided what really matters.

I. A matter of confidence
   A. Eternal confidence (v. 13)
      1. Those who are eager to do good
      2. Those who are aware of real good (Rom. 8:28)
      3. Those who are secure in the one who is good (vv. 29–30)
   B. External confidence (1 Peter 3:14)
      1. The popular principle of pain and pleasure
      2. The spiritual principle of righteousness and reward
   C. Internal confidence (v. 15)
      1. The entrance of Christ in the heart
      2. The enthronement of Christ in the heart
      3. The enjoyment of Christ in the heart

II. A matter of conviction (v. 15)
   A. Christian confidence will provoke inquiry
      1. From anyone
      2. At anytime
   B. Christian conviction must produce explanation
      1. A definition of terms is necessary
      2. A defense of position is mandatory
         a. Peter's alertness to opportunity at Pentecost (Acts 2)
         b. Peter's readiness to speak before the Sanhedrin (Acts 4)
   C. Christian concern must project esteem
      1. Projecting esteem for man
         a. Giving the question the consideration it demands
         b. Affording the questioner the opportunity he deserves
      2. Projecting esteem for God
         a. To represent God is awesome
         b. To present gospel is burdensome

III. A matter of conscience (1 Peter 3:16)
   A. Conscience is a God given faculty
      1. Intelligence can distinguish between true and false
      2. Conscience must distinguish between good and bad
      3. Will must decide on basis of the above
   B. Conscience is sin-seared and faulty
      1. The starving of conscience from lack of truth
      2. The smothering of conscience through bad decisions
      3. The searing of conscience through planned denial
   C. Conscience is a lifesaving factor
      1. When honored
      2. When honed
      3. When heeded

63

Suffering

1 Peter 3:17-22

The magnitude of human suffering is beyond understanding, and its meaning is no less challenging. But Christians, because they have a unique relationship with the crucified Savior, have a special approach to the whole subject.

I. Insight into Christ's sufferings (vv. 18–19)
   A. His sufferings were foreordained (1:10; see Luke 24:26; Acts 3:18)
   B. His sufferings were propitiatory–"for sins"
   C. His sufferings were substitutionary–"just for unjust"
   D. His sufferings were conclusive–"once for all"
   E. His sufferings were reconciliatory–bring us to God
   F. His sufferings were extraordinary–"put to death"
   G. His sufferings were temporary–"made alive"
   H. His sufferings were declaratory–"preached"
   I. His sufferings were preparatory–"resurrection"

II. Identification with a suffering Christ (1 Peter 3:20–21)
   A. The illustration of the flood
      1. The sin of man

        2. The inevitability of judgment
        3. The grace of God
        4. The building of the ark
        5. The salvation of the few
    B. The implications of baptism
        1. The flood an "antitype" of baptism
           a. The water was death to some
           b. The water was life to others
           c. The cross spells condemnation to some
           d. The cross means life to others
        2. Baptism the pledge of a good conscience
           a. Cleansed through the blood of Christ
           b. Justified by the resurrection of Christ
           c. Incorporated into the body of Christ
           d. Baptized as a commitment to Christ

III. Involvement in the suffering of Christ
    A. Christians suffer because of antagonism to Christ
    B. Christians suffer because they take stands against evil
    C. Christians suffer because they fall into sin
    D. Christians suffer because they live in a fallen world
    E. Christians suffer because of God's will (v. 17)
        1. To prove faith genuine (1:7; e.g., Job)
        2. To glorify God (1:7)
        3. To make us strong (5:10)
        4. To lead the way for mankind (4:17)

64

Facing the Cross

1 Peter 4:1-6

When Jesus said, "Anyone who does not take up his cross and follow me is not worthy of me," Peter was among the disciples who were listening. He did not understand the significance of these words at that time, but later in his epistles he shares what the Master meant.

I. The appreciation of the cross as experienced by Peter
   A. Peter's reaction to Christ (John 1:14–42)
      1. He was happy to be introduced
      2. He was prepared to be involved
   B. Peter's rejection of the cross
      1. He was appalled at the thought (Matt. 16:21–22)
      2. He was opposed to the action (John 18:10–11)
   C. Peter's reception of Calvary
      1. Peter's denial (Matt. 26:69ff.)
      2. Peter's defection
      3. Peter's delight (John 21:15ff.)
   D. Peter's reflection on the crucifixion
      1. Shown in his apostolic preaching (Acts 2:36–38)
      2. Shown in his pastoral teaching (1 Peter 3:18)

II. The application of the cross as explained by Peter
   A. Applying the cross to your attitudes (4:1)
      1. Christ died for sin
      2. Christ is done with sin
      3. I died with Christ
      4. I need to be done with sin
   B. Applying the cross to your ambitions (v. 2)
      1. Embarking on the rest of your life
      2. Embracing the best for your life
         a. The evil desires of mankind
         b. The perfect will of God
   C. Applying the cross to your activities (v. 3)
      1. The choices you made
      2. The consequences you suffered
         a. Iniquity
         b. Impurity
         c. Idolatry
      3. The changes you institute
   D. Applying the cross to your associations (v. 4)
      1. Those who lack spiritual discernment
      2. Those who lack self-discipline
      3. Those who lack simple decency

III. The appeal of the cross as expressed by Peter (vv. 5–6)
   A. Appearing in the court of the judge
      1. Those who live and are alive
      2. Those who died and live
      3. Those who live and are dead
      4. Those who died and are dead
   B. Appealing to the cross of Jesus
      1. Those who died with him will live with him
      2. Those who live through him will reign with him

65

Living Near the End

1 Peter 4:7-11

Peter was particularly conscious of the limited time available to him. This affected the way he lived, and he sought to share both this consciousness and the response with his contemporaries. His words are relevant to Christians of all generations.

    I. Christian belief concerning the end
        A. The Jewish understanding of the end (Joel 2)
        B. The disciple's questions concerning the end (Matt. 24:1-3)
        C. The apostolic preaching related to the end (Acts 2:17)
        D. The biblical teaching about the end (2 Peter 3)
            1. It is near
            2. It is in God's time
            3. It is certain
            4. It is delayed
            5. It is crucial

   II. Christian behavior considering the end
        A. Keep a cool head (4:7)

      1. Don't panic
      2. Do pray (e.g., Acts 4:23–31)
  B. Keep a steady balance (1 Peter 4:7; 2 Peter 3:8–10)
      1. Avoid the lethargy of unbelief
      2. Avoid the extremes of unbalance
  C. Keep a warm heart (1 Peter 4:8)
      1. Love–the supreme Christian virtue
      2. Love–the stretching Christian experience
      3. Love–the sheltering Christian response
  D. Keep an open house (v. 9)
      1. Houses–the center of worship
      2. Houses–the aids to mission
      3. Houses–the refuge for the needy
  E. Keep a faithful attitude (v. 10)
      1. God's grace has been distributed to all
      2. God's grace varies from person to person
      3. God's grace is given for the benefit of others
      4. God's grace is given as a trust
  F. Keep a pure message (v. 11)
      1. The privilege of hearing God's word
      2. The pleasure of doing God's word
      3. The pressure of sharing God's word
  G. Keep a powerful witness (v. 11b)
      1. The witness of being a servant of God
      2. The witness of showing the strength of God
      3. The witness of praising the Son of God

66

Handling Harsh Realities

1 Peter 4:12-19

There is a natural tendency for human beings to avoid considering the possibility that they may be required to live in difficult circumstances, and if they are confronted with such harsh realities they tend to deny the situation or evade the truth. Peter, in his difficulties, did neither, and he expected the believers to handle their harsh realities in a Christian manner.

I. Some information concerning harsh realities
   A. There is nothing strange about "fiery trials" (v. 12)
      1. A sinful world produces fiery trials
      2. A gracious God permits fiery trials
      3. A mature believer profits from fiery trials
   B. There is nothing sentimental about the "sufferings of Christ" (v. 13)
      1. The necessity of Christ's participation in a suffering world
      2. The reality of our participation in a suffering Christ

    C. There is nothing surprising about being "insulted"
       (v. 14)
       1. The name of Christ insults man's pride
       2. The pride of man insults Christ's name
       3. The bearers of the name feel the insults of the
          proud
    D. There is nothing spiritual about suffering for "wrong-
       doing" (v. 15)
       1. Illegal activities produce legal consequences
       2. Immoral activities produce moral repercussions
       3. Improper activities produce societal displeasure
    E. There is nothing shameful about being a Christian
       (v. 16)
       1. Be prepared to define the name "Christian"
       2. Be prepared to defend the name "Christian"
    F. There is nothing sacrosanct about the "family of
       God" (v. 17)
       1. The family of God is not excused from responsibility
       2. The family of God is not exempt from difficulty
       3. The family of God must expect accountability
    G. There is nothing soft about "God's will" (v. 19)
       1. "Suffering according to God's will" burns up
          dross
       2. "Suffering according to God's will" refines pure
          metal

II. Some instructions concerning harsh realities
    A. Be cheerful
       1. The cause of rejoicing (v. 13)
       2. The basis of praise (v. 16)
    B. Be content
       1. The experience of "blessedness" (v. 14)
       2. The presence of the Spirit (v. 14)
    C. Be considerate
       1. Consider relations with "those who do not obey"
          (v. 17)

    2. Consider repercussions for the "ungodly and the sinner" (v. 18)

D. Be committed

    1. The example of Christ (Luke 23:46)

    2. The confidence of the believer (2 Tim. 1:12)

E. Be consistent

    1. Being persuaded about what is good

    2. Being persistent in doing what is good

67

Take Me to Your Leaders

1 Peter 5:1-4

In all areas of human existence leadership is of the utmost importance, particularly in times of stress. It comes as no surprise, therefore, that Peter turns his attention to the leaders of the churches who are coming under pressure.

    I. The people are like sheep
        A. The weakness of sheep (Luke 15; John 10)
            1. Wild beasts
            2. Unscrupulous shepherds
            3. Natural characteristics
        B. The waywardness of sheep
            1. Peter's observation (Matt. 9:36)
            2. Peter's experience (26:31)
            3. Peter's teaching (1 Peter 2:25)

   II. The church is like the flock
        A. The concern of the Good Shepherd (John 10:14–16)
        B. The seeking of the individual (Luke 15:1–7)
        C. The establishment of the flock (12:32)

    D. The centrality of the Great Shepherd (Heb. 13:20–21)

    E. The eternal nature of the flock (1 Peter 5:4)

III. The elders are like shepherds
    A. The principle of eldership
        1. The elders of ancient Israel (Num. 11:16–17)
        2. The elders of the Roman Senate (*senex* = old man)
        3. The elders of the Sanhedrin (Luke 22:66)
        4. The elders of the synagogues
        5. The elders of the primitive churches (Titus 1:5)
    B. The practice of eldership
        1. The function of elders
            a. The shepherd function (1 Peter 5:1)
                (1) Peter's experience of the Gracious Shepherd (John 21)
                (2) Peter's witness of the Good Shepherd
                (3) Peter's reverence for the Great Shepherd
            b. The overseer function (1 Peter 5:2)
                (1) The "caring for" aspect
                (2) The "watching out for" aspect (Acts 15:36)
                (3) The "see to it" aspect (Heb. 12:15)
        2. The frailties of elders (1 Peter 5:2)
            a. Attitudes–enjoying, not enduring
            b. Motivation–love, not loot
            c. Style–models, not moguls
        3. The followership of elders (v. 5)
            a. Leadership is determined by following
            b. Followership is characteristic of discipleship

68

The Marks of Maturity

1 Peter 5:5-14

Peter's stated intention in writing this epistle was to equip the believers for tough times ahead. In conclusion he gives final instructions concerning the mature behavior he expects them to exhibit.

I. Maturity and authority (v. 5a)
   A. The role of the elder in the Christian community
   B. The response of the younger in the Christian community
   C. The recognition of authority in the Christian community

II. Maturity and humility (vv. 5b-6)
   A. Humility—the result of realistic assessment
      1. I am worth something because of creation
      2. I am worth something because of redemption
      3. I am worth something because of mission
      4. I am worth nothing apart from grace
   B. Humility—the result of rejected pride (Matt. 26:31ff.)
      1. Human pride knows better than God (v. 33)

      2. Human pride feels superior to others (v. 33)

      3. Human pride thinks grandly about self (v. 35)

      4. Human pride merits divine opposition

    C. Humility–the result of resolute action (1 Peter 5:6)

      1. The action of the apron (John 13:4ff.)

      2. The attention to one another

      3. The anticipation of exaltation

III. Maturity and anxiety (1 Peter. 5:7)

    A. Degrees of anxiety

      1. Normal anxiety that is necessary

      2. Moderate anxiety that is motivating

      3. Excessive anxiety that is enervating

    B. Discernment about anxiety

      1. God is a caring heavenly Father (see Matt. 6:25, 34)

      2. Cares must be committed to his control

IV. Maturity and sobriety (1 Peter 5:8–9)

    A. A sober assessment of the situation

      1. The external attacks of the enemy

      2. The internal response of the flesh

    B. A sober reaction to the situation

      1. Keep your wits about you

      2. Keep your desires under control

      3. Keep your feet firmly planted

      4. Keep your enemy at bay

 V. Maturity and stability (vv. 10–11)

    A. Stability through sensing the hand of God (v. 6b)

    B. Stability through seeing the call of God

      1. The call to eternal glory

      2. The call through earthly suffering

    C. Stability through standing in the grace of God

      1. The grace of God is all-sufficient

      2. The grace of God is all-strengthening

Stuart Briscoe Expository Outlines series

Expository Nuggets for Today's Christians
Expository Nuggets from Genesis and Exodus
Expository Nuggets from Psalms and Proverbs
Expository Nuggets from the Gospels
Expository Nuggets from 1 Corinthians
Expository Nuggets from the Epistles

Cassette tapes of the sermons preached from the outlines in this book are available from

TELLING THE TRUTH
P.O. Box 11
Brookfield, WI 53005